Every Goodbye Ain't G

MW01026644

Every Goodbye Ain't Gone

An Anthology of Innovative Poetry by African Americans

Edited by ALDON LYNN NIELSEN
and LAURI RAMEY

THE UNIVERSITY OF ALABAMA PRESS
Tuscaloosa

Typeface: Janson Text

∞

The paper on which this book is printed meets the minimum requirements of
American National Standard for Information Sciences-Permanence of Paper for
Printed Library Materials, ANSI Z39.48-1984.

Library of Congress Cataloging-in-Publication Data

Every goodbye ain't gone : an anthology of innovative poetry by African
Americans / edited by Aldon Lynn Nielsen and Lauri Ramey.
     p.   cm. — (Modern and contemporary poetics)
  ISBN-13: 978-0-8173-1496-5 (cloth : alk. paper)
  ISBN-10: 0-8173-1496-2 (cloth : alk. paper)
  ISBN-13: 978-0-8173-5279-0 (pbk. : alk. paper)
  ISBN-10: 0-8173-5279-1 (pbk. : alk. paper)
  1. American poetry—African American authors. 2. African Americans—Poetry.
I. Nielsen, Aldon Lynn. II. Ramey, Lauri. III. Series.
  PS591.N4E937 2006
  811.008′0896073—dc22

2005014208

Contents

Introduction
Fear of a Black Experiment

Who will enter its beautiful calligraphy of blood
Jayne Cortez

at its worst or best
every nest
is different
by the way a feather
is tucked or a straw is bent!
Melvin B. Tolson

"Who Speaks Negro?" asked Sarah Webster Fabio as recently as 1966, and while it is probably the case that such a question is read with yet more irony in our own purportedly post-ironic era, it was already an odd question in its day. Fabio was responding, of course, to the proposition put forward by Karl Shapiro in his introduction to the later work of Melvin B. Tolson that Tolson's work was somehow written in "Negro," perhaps an even more curious label than "Ebonics." Still, Fabio's argument against Shapiro was not that there was no singular tongue that could properly be termed "Negro" or "black," so much as it was an insistence that whatever "Negro" might be, Tolson's poetry was not an instance of it.

The critical counter in these disputes always seems to involve the enlistment of Langston Hughes in dubious battle. Hence, at the University of Kansas centennial conference devoted to the life and works of Langston Hughes, Onwuchekwa Jemie opposed the "folksy, populist and proletarian" verses of Hughes to the writings of those moderns whose poetry he sees as "a code needing to be cracked." It is a familiar opposition by now. In his magisterial biography of Langston Hughes, Arnold Rampersad complains in passing that Tolson, in composing his *Libretto for the Republic of Liberia*, "had written probably the most hyper-European, unpopulist poem ever penned by a black writer." Further, the biography asks, "Did it not matter that very few of the American Friends of Liberia, and even fewer Liberians themselves, could understand the poem"? There are, as it happens, any number of questions being begged in these formulations. Who among us is in a position to decide what poetry Liberians may or may not be able to understand? Would Tolson's work seem "hyper-European" to Europeans? Are there no "folksy" codes needing to be cracked? (As Tolson likes to tell us, sometimes the Africans "go esoteric" on us.) Do populism and proletarian politics imply a particularized language and poetics? If the poetry of the high moderns is a code needing to be cracked, what is that wondrous late collage of Hughes's, *Ask Your Mama*? More importantly, where is Hughes himself in all this?

We do not have far to look. In his *Chicago Defender* column for December 15, 1945, Hughes wrote an answer before the fact: "But Melvin Tolson is no highbrow. Kids from the cottonfields like him. Cowpunchers understand him." Lest it be thought that Hughes was only thinking of the earlier Tolson, we have the evidence of a later *Defender* column in which it is precisely the Tolson of *Libretto for the Republic of Liberia* that Hughes presses upon his readers. Where Rampersad is concerned that the *Libretto* might be incomprehensible to readers, Hughes recommends that volume, along with the *Lincoln University Poets Centennial Anthology*, to his *Defender* audience as books "small enough to slip easily into your bag for vacation reading, and nice to lend to other folks wherever you are going, who may have forgotten to bring a book with them."

It would seem unseemly for those of us who read after Langston Hughes to be less capacious and more captious in our critique than he was, and he was a tireless promoter of even the outer reaches of African American experimentation—witness the wide net he set in editing *New Negro Poets U.S.A.*, or his friendship with the poets of the Free Lance Workshop in Cleveland, particularly their most eccentric experimentalist, Russell Atkins. Hughes contributed to the early issues of the *Free Lance* journal and was among its more avid readers. When Atkins sent Hughes a copy of his phenomenal *Phenomena*, exactly the sort of book some would dismiss as code needing to be cracked, Hughes responded enthusiastically and, in typical fashion, supplied Atkins the addresses for two other young black poets he thought would be interested, LeRoi Jones and Gloria Oden. That Hughes saw a kinship between his own efforts and the emerging innovations of Atkins's group is evidenced by

Hughes's mention in that same letter of excerpts from *Ask Your Mama* that he was offering to *Free Lance* for first publication. Just two weeks after this letter was posted, Hughes devoted a section of his *Defender* column's book recommendations to Atkins's strange volume:

> One of the foremost of our avant-garde poets, Russell Atkins of Cleveland, a member of the Free Lance group there, has published at the Wilberforce University Press a most unusual collection of drama-poems, "PHENOMENA." Wilberforce is to be congratulated for bringing out such a highly original and unconventional chapbook. Afro-American academic institutions usually pay little attention to poetry, even of the conventional sort. When the poetry is as personal as that of Atkins, unusual in both form and subject matter, its publishers must indeed be commended for giving readers the privilege of seeing it. In Atkins's poetry the mood if not always the meaning reaches out and hits you. And who always knows what anything—even the simplest things—mean? Do you?

The late Stephen Henderson, a critic who cast his nets well beyond the fished-out waters of the main stream, argued that African American music:

> is not afraid of new philosophies or new technologies; for the music deals with time filtered through the pulses of African sensibility. So no ideological hangup should prevent Black poets from writing "sound poems," especially with the model of Bob Kaufman, and Ella Fitzgerald, Louis Armstrong, and the moaning of the Baptist preacher.

Though poets of sparkling originality and theoretical sophistication, Atkins and his Free Lance collaborators are part of a larger context of African American mid-century poetic experimentalists, including others who were promoted by Hughes. Calvin C. Hernton, another Hughes protégé, moved to the Lower East Side of New York in 1961. Here Hernton came into contact with other black literary innovators whose idiom—both black and reflecting modern and early postmodern trends (significantly, not an oxymoron)—was located at the intersection of poetry, music, art, politics, and performance. The stylistic and social ferment lighting up that time and place were in part the inheritance of the interracial, cross-arts dynamism of international modernism. That same year, seeking to establish a group of artists to encourage one another's work, Hernton co-founded The Society of Umbra. Participants in the Umbra workshops, performances, and magazine included David Henderson, Ishmael Reed, Lloyd Addison, Norman Pritchard, and Lorenzo Thomas.

Hernton's poetry foregrounds performative features such as hypnotic rhythm, complex echoic patterns of repetition, and references to African American culture. Ballads and blues poems in his collection *Medicine Man* echo Sterling Brown and Hughes in using a folk-based aesthetic (including musical idioms, especially blues, jazz, and spirituals) to create sophisticated African American cultural portraits. His extended lyrics such as the collection's title poem, which formally are rhythm-driven fragmentary patchworks, reflect a dizzying array of homely and erudite references, showing the influence of Melvin B. Tolson as much as T. S. Eliot. For Hernton and others, the search for an authentic voice as an African American poet included being aware of the developments of modernism and its implications for black culture. In fact, these influences are embraced and insisted on by many African American poetic innovators of the era, in sharp contrast with the image of rather inward-looking cultural isolation sometimes implied by the canon. Another pocket of similar innovation in the form of an avant-garde collective was the somewhat better known Dasein poets, which included Percy Johnston.

But what fate awaits these poets who propose to write from the fullest range of African American sensibilities?

"This proposal does not pass the significance test." With these dismissive words, one outside reviewer (the only one rendering a negative opinion) advised the National Endowment for the Humanities to reject a proposal from Hampton University made in association with work on this anthology. The proposed project had as its chief goal the preservation of the works of poets such as those of the Dasein/Howard group, the Free Lance group and the Umbra associates. The reviewer proceeded to comment that "the rescuing, preservation, and dissemination of everything cannot occur. A pecking order is necessary." Of course, the proposal writers had never suggested that every poet needs to be canonized, nor even the more modest proposal that these particular poets should each be canonized, let alone that all poetry ever written should always be preserved for study. But what the reviewer's comment reveals more nakedly than is normal is the aggressive tone so often adopted by defenders of a canon that should not be in need of defense. Were it the case that literary works enter the canon as the result of their eternal appeal to universal human qualities, then the canon should survive quite well on its own without heroic measures to prevent competition. One thing is certain, if poems are kept from collection and held at arm's length from the syllabi of literary study, they will not be canonized, but neither will readers of the canon be in any position to comprehend the historical context in which their own readings proceed.

All poets anticipate readers, but few of the poems gathered here were written with palpable designs upon the canon. Still, there were readers, some of whom became champions of the new poetries emerging in the decades after the second World War. In 1954, Hughes wrote to Russell Atkins to congratulate him on the planned opera Atkins was to create with composer Hale Smith. Hughes went on to speak enthusiastically about the small press magazine Atkins was editing at the time: "I hear that there is a new issue of THE FREE LANCE, and that you have some penetrating poetical comments on some other poets' work in it. Please send me a copy." Whatever was happening within the classrooms and anthologies of mid-century mid-America, black poets were addressing themselves to one another, creating corresponding anthologies across each other's writing desks.

As readers neared the close of the poetry section in *The Negro Caravan*, the 1941 gathering of African-American literature edited by Sterling Brown, Arthur P. Davis, and Ulysses Lee, they encountered works by Robert Hayden and Melvin B. Tolson that signaled the coming of the radical new poetries that would appear in the decades following the second World War. By 1964 Langston Hughes's *New Negro Poets U.S.A.* gave evidence of a far-reaching revolution in aesthetics and prosody mounted by black poets throughout the United States, some working independently and others in consciously constructed groups. Meanwhile, in the contiguous republics of America represented by Norton, Heath, MacMillan and the syllabi of historically white universities and colleges, none of this was yet visible. Stephen Henderson has recently argued that, even during a period of increased critical attentions to African American literature, "the Black writers of the 1960s and early 1970s who created some of the most moving and challenging literature of our time have scarcely received any critical or scholarly attention at all."

Looking at the best-known literary anthologies of the late forties, fifties, and early sixties, a reader simply might not know that the breakthroughs of Hayden, Brooks, Tolson, and others had been followed by dozens of new poets who journeyed to the outermost possibilities of prosody. In the sixties and seventies, groups of poets appeared in anthologies, often edited by other poets, who did much to force a re-examination of the canons of American verse. Following in the wake of the Black Arts Movement, numerous anthologies appeared that, like Hughes's *New Negro Poets*, put before readers the stunning breadth of poetries composed by African Americans. In the space of a few years the list of widely available collections included: *We Speak as Liberators, The New Black Poetry, Soulscript, Dices or Black Bones, Black Fire, The Poetry of Black America, The Black Poets, For Malcolm, You Better Believe It*, and *Understanding the New Black Poetry. You Better Believe It*, edited by Paul Breman and published in 1973, even went so far as to presciently place some of the boldest African American poetry in an international context. This anthology sketched one of the earliest portraits of an avant-garde, diasporic dialogue by placing figures such as Tolson, Kaufman, Atkins, Joans, Addison, Baraka, Spellman, Major, Reed, Pritchard, Fields, Henderson, and Hernton (surely suggesting a counter-canonical canon based on that listing alone) head-to-head with Christopher Okigbo, Edward Brathwaite, Dennis Brutus, Kofi Awoonor, Wole Soyinka, Mukhtarr Mustapha, John La Rose, Dennis Scott, Ama Ata Aidoo, and Keorapetse Kgositsile. With such a wealth of anthologies being perused by so many, it was inevitable that the volumes designed primarily for the academic market would begin to reflect, in however small a way, some few signs of this outpouring. Soon enough, collections devoted to the history of American literature that had presented their texts as a white mythology in all prior editions suddenly found room within their commodious pages for an occasional Brooks or Baraka. But the door opened only far enough to allow one or two access, affirmative or otherwise, to the halls of academe, and then the doors shut tightly against many who had forced them open in the first place. Having knocked at the door that a Hayden should enter, many found that was as much as most mainstream anthologies could seem to contemplate. Tolson often proved too . . . something. Baraka came to serve synecdochically for all black experiment, and the pure plain surface of identitarian free verse, occasionally enlivened by the presence of a New Afro-Neo-Formalist, came to be all of that long, black song that America could hear singing. Though the plethora of black poetry anthologies of the sixties and seventies had done so much to open the American university curriculum to black writing, the more adventurous of black lyric was all too often silenced.

But, "every goodbye ain't gone." Despite what you've been reading, there's more and better reading. In the past few years a number of anthologies have appeared even more expansive in their vision than the enlarged canon of today's classroom. In E. Ethelbert Miller's *In Search of Color Everywhere* we can again read A. B. Spellman, Tom Dent, Calvin Forbes, and Elouise Loftin. Clarence Major, who edited *The New Black Poetry* against such unthinking resistance in 1969 has now produced *The Garden Thrives*, in which he returns to public view such poets as the now much neglected Russell Atkins, Julia Fields, David Henderson, Ed Roberson, Lorenzo Thomas, and Tom Weatherly. And Jerry Ward's historical survey of African-American poetry, *Trouble the Water*, has been released. In his editor's preface Ward makes the simple, direct, and common-sensical observation, one that has been ignored by almost all American literature anthologies when they come to the representations of black verse, that "Before one canonizes on the literary/extraliterary axis, it seems desirable to represent the variety and difference that actually does exist." The actually existing variety with which Ward troubles the placid waters of today's multiculti anthology market encompasses such truly troubling poets as Bob Kaufman, Tom Dent, Julia Fields, Clarence Major, David Henderson, Lorenzo Thomas, and Harryette Mullen.

If the American publishing industry and its attendants in the academy appear to have slept through much of the poetic ferment in black America across the past three decades, Michael Harper and Anthony Walton were there, like Ward, Miller, and Major, to remind us that *Every Shut Eye Ain't Asleep*. What has been missing from view since about 1972, though, has been the iceberg whose tip trips up the New Critical ship of fools who, like the anonymous reviewer assuring us that not all poets need to be reread, want to steer us safely to the shores of an unassuming blackness, a blackness bathed in the white light of canonical benevolence. That iceberg is a free-floating signifier of black experiment; it's what raises the water that floats our boat; it's the sign at sea that reminds us, far from port, that "every goodbye ain't gone."

Anthologies may be read as simultaneous gestures of greeting and exclusion. While the editors make no pretense to encyclopedic coverage of avant-garde, black poetics from the decades following the Second World War, we continue to feel the deepest regret as we reread poems that we are not able to include here. Some artists elected not to be included. Some bodies of work are surrounded by legal difficulties of considerably greater complexity than the verse itself. Some readers will no doubt think we have elided a crucial candidate. The gathering assembled here might best be regarded as a preliminary sketch, intended to entice and intended as invitation to further readings and incitements. There will be more to come, but for now, we offer this collection as a means of remapping the ground in ways that may shift our historical comprehensions of African American poetry in recent years and our anticipations of critical comprehensions to come. The present collection affords a fresh perspective on the more experimental poetries created by African American artists in the decades following the Second World War. A planned subsequent volume will carry these representations forward into the years and movements that followed. One of the anonymous readers for this anthology project performed an interesting bit of calculation. Examining the ratio of female-to-male contributors represented in *Black Fire*, perhaps the most broadly influential anthology representing the Black Arts Movement, our reader found that editors Larry Neal and Amiri Baraka had produced a collection in which just 9 percent of the poets were women. The percentage of women contributors in *Every Goodbye Ain't Gone* is approximately twice that number. We wish that it could have been even higher, but again, we were not successful in securing poems from all of the potential contributors we approached. Still, it is important to recognize that the proportions of male and female contributors in *published* collections during the time period we here survey was typified by the numbers we see in *Black Fire*. Surely this is not to say that many more women artists weren't actively pursuing the more adventurous avenues of poetic composition. (Indeed, mainstream poetry shows no better record of gender equality during this period.) Rather, it is a sign of the barriers that still existed in a literary world dominated by men. One of the most important things we can do today is to recognize the importance of those such as Jayne Cortez, Elouise Loftin, Gloria Tropp, and June Jordan who broke a path for the many women who were to come after them, the remarkable next generation of women artists whose work will reappear in the next installment of this project.

Every new reading requires a break from the established disciplinary modes, a break from regnant pecking orders, and a breakthrough. The lone negator among Hampton University's NEH referees remarked that "projects dealing with subjects now deemed minor in a humanistic context are regularly passed over in favor of others whose importance is manifest." "Will the circle be unbroken?" asks one of the editors of this collection. "Give us a break," responds the more contentious.

We trust we will not be alone in seeking such a break. We hope that this collection will stand as another, more munificent means of making manifest. For Black American poets, contesting the taken for granted is no new task. One purpose of this anthology is precisely to raise questions about the manifest importance of work in whose favor poems such as these "are regularly passed over." There is another passing over, and there is a better reading on the other side. As Atkins writes in "At Night Keep Still":

There are, everywhere unheard
(as one might see deep in an electron microscope)
rigidities
          violently breaking

Where some might want to dismiss such stanzas as codes in need of cracking, we might do better to ask, with Langston Hughes, the question that is everywhere implicit in the writing of Russell Atkins, "who always knows what anything—even the simplest things—mean? Do you?" We might respond with Hughes to those who would keep such texts from a wider audience, to those who insist on a pecking order that would obscure from view most of what goes on between these covers: "Ask your mama."

LLOYD ADDISON

I by you put on

Knew you upon the one true time
              two   to times   shifting
being too badly moved in mood
to come to see me born again to be something born of you
                            much a part of heart-felt two
                                    you should be
                                    slightly half of me
                  in part and place of you

though only partly placing one
                without my really being half
                but having here something truly in the place of time
                                and thought having you instead
                                feeding one feeling-view to want
                      bathed in me
                      water and water and watermellow
                      shower and well-cool and felt fellow

is by the I put on
                  the dress of something haunted
                              by the near untrue
                  in the Gypsy hour of fortune-telling
                  all of a feeling incomplete

After MLK:

the marksman marked leftover kill

Until deaf-dumb bullet self-improved comi-tragic time
deathdrops suicidally from error of unimproved trajectory
towards humankind's disintegrating vestpocket protest suitability,
and its ex-it disappear-ring of steel rearbounds
for vain deathproof namesake gods,
watch the little black hole
in the new world order undeliver-rated life-space;

if execution equals solution, let beforesight exceed
where mass meetings equal civilly engineered rights
obversely proportional to wishfountainpen power,
and anti-rights-bodies equal ten/time square
by the co-efficient light minus the magnetic exponential . . .

and if the short straight pigskin pass between All-American equals
the short straight bullet line pass to Other-Americannots—
on an elect/rode day-o shootout in atomic space-limited time—
into how many bullblooded pointillistic pigments
will the first canvass camped war of the worlds explode awry?

Hereby youth articles of war a unifying field threat
to destruct distrust-overlapping generations past
to inherit their time of health to live,
or run on sentence-structured fellowship.mad theme antics,
ordering inapt peeled evil bitterthick
to eat the beauty fall indigestion limbo, Armageddon Eve,
a surfeit's indefinite period . . .

and THOU SHALT NOT not KILL ROYALTY
was here latrined behind these walls where maddog stood,
and dog said let there be muzzle velocity
and there was a ballistics report of delight,

enriched, the eye-witness to the creation of death said,
man his tri-vestry of cloth-skintightrope walked
when he should have crawled—will vindicate me . . .
whether in Kings or Psalms or Ecclesiastes,
never blink, in Acts or Revelation:
by goods the goodbye contract of the little black hole.

And as for the law of inertia,
concern with man-condition will elect trick cutie state rights
obtaining arrears rest warrants for perpetual motion aliases
fleeing ten-to-twenty delight years of overfunny

So now rhetoric unpacked good physics call forth overcoming:
uni-lateral-field anti-hymns of Ptolemaic tickled bylaws,
with march-on strike for ghetto respect and labor,
in Copernican accounting for a new toned iron sting in graft itches
before the picture of muzzle simultaneously develops
to mass spree-the-corpuscle of dropout entropic delight,
to wRap tRap white nightrider wind in Brown paperbags for sailing . . .

All the things of which there are none

Among all the things of which there are none
        I'll have a little bit of play widt / with having
                that one / full body of knowledge

Here with we will open buds
      & scatter seeds far as are accountings

And they are millions of kings
these seeds that rush fro/from thither kingdoms come

         who have been king-size-excited runners-up
         & others to manfully affirm in/thru
         the little white-legged spot thin slipper

& herein is our campaign of love of that ecstatic nevermind
             possessed of wet-torched body
in a demon's/straight.manipulation democracy of the humid race

& 3-dimensioned tired twin inner-truthless compunctioned blowouts
       appeal to blowup/down inner outburst
         holding at knowledge's intense dependent foresight
       against head'sache to peek at
         the on-climbing explosion of high octangency
      with shouting perfection
      prompted to speak of cue-t-countdown
'where the performance of a second second
         programs to split open
         deadaheadlines to egg-scramble am/bushwoman

And all the things of which there are none
         in milk bottles stooped / necking instructions
         for white hippopotamus health & cow cud rentals

cricketly picked from a witchcraftsman's handbag
become the noble salvage

All the things of which there are none
in disconnection make no-man's landlady's pocket book

where bets around blow up to midnight's morning flat
to forgive a debt's receipt informally foresaid

& with a clean body/snatch-cheer
the lovebugkiller ladykiller is in-putout
& all the things of witches are done to night

to have a spine-spillover joy-enthralled
dark end day over all day
cultivating green stem-merged nervous systematic kilocalories

& without & out aboutface fit of onset values
here to go/aheadway-off in the fact chimera
to have a flair O-well lonesome
until reveling laid
to a peeled-off out-of-work wonder fill-in

the good peel hysterically off
& all the things of which there are nonetheless
the main asideway-farers' refreshment understanding

Umbra

My sun has gone down in drum suite penumbra
The mood of this rhythm my body is umbra

And the totem line behind the three-faced light tabu
        decline the flesh-cup curve

The postmen ask
What information in address envelops this female
                              impertinence
                              posturing behind us

      this is not thigh ten-inch-pound distance weight focus
      this is the weight of death
             full to fascination bottom riddle end but dense
      one face-frontal curve
      or straight instantline   say designers of fashion
            no rear view is beautiful to address
                     but to the self
      one clean brief declension
            is to write to inform and to clothe to invite
This is the interval of a question addressing the male
The umbral body is in penumbral field
                  a two-way cup curving female
        a handful of image an armsful storm
            a mouthy world waiting

And the lips that kiss you in penumbra have arms
A body molds the darkness is thigh-pressed cradle-abdomen met
        and breasts the umbral breasts have softness

And the silence neuter feminine night
        is sighing verb-breaths to love

And handsome she has fingers to caress herself down
      circular the darkness is erect

feverish at its back the stars perspire
pressed to her back the hands of the arms that engulf her
                                        hold her enrapt
            cool lips press against her throat
erect the darkness is spinning in an arc PM space
                a perpendicular in its equator
                a right angle in its tropics lights
erect the darkness stands
                goes gentle merry-go-round in the wheel
                            with a rub in the trouble hub
                            the axle oil gives ease

spoke
                said muffled mute hot gerund to be is being is
                            the night pitch
                            the feeling pic

                            love is a good gentle cut

            between thin spreads of dough its meats
            the kneading spirit is gripped

            and the handle in this feeding time
            equipped with potfat floodlight milk
                    to go roaring to the royal pitch pond
            is to the self-darkness square root
                the set formula to be feeling figure-field

The fall from the shoulders
careening down the umbral back
            the act of line arcs
                    moving to divide hill

                    And the black thumb of its beauty
is an index figure written in sand
and five fathomables of a handful in a swim

is a catch
a watery whim which sets and vanishes addressed

                laughing out of a darkness fluent with light
                and lonely

speeding round in plus-diamond closure
breaking refraction naked
little jewels of blackbrown white darkness
cutting colors of weightlight to pair   to explode
compound the inner spectrum under surface-limited line

This body's conjunctive curcuit is
on somnambulant current continuance of attraction

Into the flow of this river tittering ruthlessly
of having being going broken rhythm at middle emotion flood
a gurgle in the whirlpool erring eye at thigh/s/ hips' concourse
Cleanses a touch of kinesthesia

handful of the hollow space-solid stomach

a time envelope distended fretfully lolling to tension
that hands move over leaving the mouth deliciously weak
hands move to clutch that having being
to handle mouth's pout from distant touch
thigh raised to handsome cup

In violable twilight feeling
she wins watching   the gaited dance

Her hair is lacklustre black justnight
a vapor porous posy potted in relief
sculptured to a mating cloud growing wild

her forehead is arched in appositive poise
prominent in majestic sweep
conceding to her lips that she O is
kiss is love

her eyes seed lightdrunk aura light's winter moons
are aura and aura cool light afire

her face is a slope swelling at the lips
touched with a pink of sunset evenly fading dark
nourished warm of watt to love ethos

turning out well thirst to will thirst
where love drinks love looks full-lipped fat handsome water pinks
to give a full smooth smiling peal

WILLIAM ANDERSON

There's Not a Friend like the Lowly Jesus

Suddenly, against the mountainous
wall of the fireplace,
soot begins to glow.

At the ocean
at that very moment,
the waves spread their lips.
In the folds of the sierra

nevada, a crowd
of skiers rides down the snow.
They hold torches, they
wave and shout, so you can hear
them in the
hotel.

If you're in any way
a prophet, you
better figure why a nigger
is different from yourself, or any

of the above lights. Because when I
think of all the things
I do to keep from

dying.

RUSSELL ATKINS

It's Here in the

Here in the newspaper — wreck of the East Bound.
A photograph bound to bring on cardiac asthenia.
There is a blur that mists the pages:
On one side's a gloom of dreadful harsh,
Then breaks flash lights up sheer.
There is much huge about, I suppose
      those no's are people
     between that suffering of—
      (what have we more? for Christ's sake!
Something of a full stop of it
crash of blood and the still shock
       of stark sticks and an immense swift gloss
And two dead no's lie aghast still
One casts a crazed eye and the other's
     closed dull
        the heap twists up
     hardening the unhard, unhardening
     the hardened

Probability and Birds

The probability in the yard:
The rodent keeps the cat close by;
The cat would sharp at the bird;
The bird would waft to the water—
If he does he has but his times before.
Whichever one he is he's surely marked

The cat is variable
The rodent becomes the death of the bird
Which we love
          dogs are random

While Waiting for a Friend to Come to Visit a Friend in a Mental Hospital

eyes thieve with prickled stir:
the attendant has ideas about me

the attendant keeps watch, watching
that abrupt wild uranium grow a bat's ears,
sardine flowers, moon's eggs,
                            stomach guitars,
a double-bass rump—but he's err:
one shrews to his inferences,
here where the world's sharp'd
sheen'd across with antiseptic spear

always be afar if it is challenge,
the off-shores of the eyes direct
devilishly in this "catch me" business

I have about the least to do
with white-coated attendants,
                    soft'd thither nurses,
and the sleep particles—

stop looking
            (—a friend's gone banking
and I'm waiting
            that is all

Spyrytual

Oh didn't it """   """""   """""
           ""   ""
           ""   ""
           ""   ""
                  "
""   "
 ""
    ""
    ""   ""

  rain
    ""
       ""
    ""   ""   ""

Oh did
  """"" """""   n't   ""
  ""
        ""   it
 rain
    ""
    ""

Lines in Recollection

I had just arrived on the advanced slope and I

did think of Grant Woods and some others:

                         no trouble at all

to see the around'd spanned circular far

moving hills orbed exciting sweep

there the coy farm settled heavy shapes

th' uproarious trees of startlingly beautious flowers!

the L_____   L   L
        oN G   ON G   ON   G place
                               S   e

L   L   L   L
   O n) G ONg)   ON G L oNg

place   that   PLACE

    TH'   ONe   g'd
                L   place
L   u N   OnE
Un
ouNOUN   _____
   g   /_____ /_____

                       _____/
                  1
         _____/   moving .

Furious'd Garb

The across and rain of away. I took shred of an umbrella
                              Furious'd garb.
My key into the lock went dare.
Like whoms the house, the fence, the door, the gate!
A grave's lo! where I did fate, flew fluff'd!
"If ye be, ye far excited, authenticate!"

The street came down with fantastic!
Blast furnace wonderous'd the air with grisly spirit!
Pale blown aside of out, extinguishable moon.
There! Mrs. Rhone forth'd, briefly—
Shroud of hers by crypt? (no, No.
I mistook. Light of lamp.)

                              Furious'd garb.

Listen: More spoken of "reality"
and face to face with it as the at desk
at ink at phone at typewriter
and business'd in coat and tie, et al., sons & co.

and we will think it much to go
from that window into aghasts below!

Night and a Distant Church

Forward abrupt   up
then mmm mm
wind mmm m
      mmm   m
upon
the mm mmm
wind mmm m
      mmm
into the mm wind
rain now and again
the mm wind
bells
    bells

Christophe

Upstood upstaffed
                    passing sinuously away over an airy arch
          streaming where all th' lustres
          streaming
                    sinuously shone
          bright
                    where more sky
Upstood upstaffed
                    th' sumptuously ready
          flags full—
          (th' shaded soothed an' blowing softly
          th' underlings smoothly
          with horses
                    wavering with winds
tangling with manly manners
                              thick
gathering th' steeds)
                    that
forthwith
up up
Christophe
appearing in th' imminent
an th' passion overjoying the hour
unfolded
          flaming
Highly th' imperial sign
shone in his glory

Irritable Songs

1
some meaning rain
between by-walls
where woebegone
and ashcans misery

thunder's refrain
(lung's phlegm
for a gutter):
a hush afters

in the wan room
of afternoon
        one feels,
intuitively, the refragable

too late

2

       convalescing:
drear'd with ill   there lay
the debris of vulnerability,
lapsed books, newspapers
lying like recoil

      adrift abed

or part of a lifeboat
extraneous at the ends
of a watery tether?

      a dugout
compiled to the neck
in sand?

3

                          be ready
to drink Borgia   or ablaze
thwart to the brain   and/or
hurl through uproar   through sheer
the very body
                    calamitous'd
blunted about the hard pavement
                    guts out:

                    or

take despair as a car
(as in the cinema)
chasm'd to a crash abrupt'd in fire!
          strewn so to extremes!
or dirge to a lake
eved for your thirst—
your thirst for
ever

4
shock the bastards:
eschew employment and the years
of such employment's benefits:
Social Security and Credit Unions
Retirement Funds, Insurances!
amidst recession, quit a job
and lack payments and credit cards!
here's another: go through
hospitals and have x-rays
or a complete checkup

then wait
            for the collection agency!

5

the squat figure that comes with concern
who has so much concern   see,
but wait for someone bringing, bringing

and for some the world brings more:
when there are oranges, quilts, quinine,
it will bring oranges, quilts, quinine
—the world brings more, brings,
never stops bringing

but for another?
            see, then, who comes low
in through the appurtenances,
who has so much concern
—the figure, squat, hissing
that comes with concern

6

horror of sunset stealths
through the boughs of birch:
sunk in a sigh the whole nauseous red:
the sun's hideous liquid
fills gutters   frantic
the twigs at the window—
away goes through the air,
old cans abject   by-ways whimper
                    —the night sky's
at its death-fall

7

perpetual stales, wearies, olds;
ambition yores behind—
there is of on and wayside,
traffic slowly eternals itself
into distance   familiarity
coins more commonplaces:
such are these days!

some slivers of aspiration?
stir of a wish?

a wraith waving a grey scarf

Narrative

I sat with John Brown.   That night moonlight framed
  the blown of his beard like a portent's undivulged.
He came and said "It's Harper's, men!"

Now Harper's was a place in which death thousand'd
  for us!
Already our faces, even as he told of how,
  sweated.   And then suddenly, he,
with fierced spark'd eye—incredible heavens!

Horses dreadful appearance had of exhumed:
  our boots strode the ready. We dared off.

As generally seeming of the trail!
  smooth—and so whist!
  i.e., save sounded thunder
  of us in a rush
  passed swift fierce"ft
  'ierce shsh!!
  'ss'd in a w'isk!
  'ierced passed "ft!
Harper's a!p!p!e!a!r!e!d!
  —into it we went in a dust!

"ft passed 'ierced
  "if's, in, ss'd
  shsh "erced
  "ft
  "isk

At Night Keep Still

After-twelve   darkly comes back full stop,
                hush about slumberers.
There's an accompanying negating
                intelligence:
some other will.   Take the cupboards:
in them, resistances, odd assortments,
Bruegel spiteful in the dishes;
next, autonomous hands in the fragile ether,
a frolicking of silences:
cuss of a crash that spills—
                collect the vocal glass!

I go soft about it—slumber,
chairs devil the way of hushes
                thwarting caution
—some sibilance in the radiator
amplifying

draw water, havoc the old plumbing,
a consternation of its whole network

There are, everywhere unheard
(as one might see deep in an electron microscope)
rigidities
      violently breaking

Imaginary Crimes in a Real Garden

a spring already short of breath
on its way to asthma'd summer:
                    I gather
allergic grass and shrubs' roots
sterile from last year (no rainfall'll)
help them no hope from water)
                    useless beseech by boughs:
a blueberry bush asking, pleading;
faggots in a bunch, their necks,
snap of twigs' necks   crunched!
                    thick earth—
between the hands, against the knuckles
(a fat man's squeezed trachea)
a bough woman's fetus,
a shape of a female twig
                    break her
                    scream of rape
slow, painful
a feminine squirming
                    I shove
them down   bind the bag
with a short wire
                    this is the kill

AMIRI BARAKA

Biography

Hangs.
whipped
blood
stripped
meat pulled
clothes ripped
slobber
feet dangled
pointing
noised
noise
churns
face
black sky
and moon
leather night
red
bleeds
drips
ground
sucks
blood
hangs
life wetting
sticky
mud

laughs
bonnets
wolfmoon
crazyteeth

hangs

hangs

granddaddy
granddaddy, they tore

his
neck

The violence of the mind is the violence of God

Actual killing actual death the hanging the beating the running into fire
the violence of reality is the violence of the unseen the spirit
charging flesh with not being spirit hacks it open birds and great almighty
Jesus die like live live like are like and the similarity is the complex of all
    [being
We are all in the mind of God in the mind of God is the mind of God
    [which
is the flexing Olorun driving drifting climbing into blazing heaven,
    [forehead
touching the earth. We are in the mind of Shaitan, our whisperer the
    [deadly
white consciousness the other the alternate to Good, where it lay on the
    [street
nodding in prayer
Till the sky changes
and the sign is to move
and they do, the righteous, the billions of them
blacker than anything but God
do move, and their motion, is the horde drum
in the bush, the wind bathing the mountain, all the sounds of the universe
and those out beyond, is the motion, the moving, the stilleto swift doing

How People Do

To be that weak lonely figure
coming home through the cold
up the stairs
melting in grief
the walls and footsteps echo
so much absence and ignorance
is not to be the creature emerging
into the living room, an orderly universe
of known things all names and securely placed
is not to be the orderer the namer, the stormer
and creator, is not to be that, so we throw it
from our minds, and sit down casually
to eat

The Heavy

For RC

Eye is static, the guns bebopping too
close for statement, cannot be seen
bullets rattling and ramming, scaring
philosophy. But you see, and are hyp
notized. So that talking, language
lifts you, above the common or the
real. And you make a room of darkness,
and claim what you see is Lord.

Lefty

Go
home, drop, go, back
tired weather lulls, go
staggered almost, homes where they sit
smoking away, burning down to black crisps

Go,
        down, the low blows, make me into things
        any time we see, another lady come into
        the room. His eyes panted. So thin she never
        came again, except the roof where drawers
        lower than blows, wd the wind, drag the fogs
        away.
                Communication of the sign.
                By the treaty maker.
                Communication of the shore's
                design.
                By the children of caution.
                His girls run along the sea side
                dreaming of his songs. Wave echo.
                Light on off, bird streak at night.
                Coasts shifting, lined endeavor, from
                green to liver sick mountains too bored
                to become a desert.

Go, be, an interval. A sign. Their shiftless
tired faces. Black sweat, in the moon fixed.
Amble, shamble, dissemble, gamble, love's own.
Lie to them. Hurt me, quickly. Love's a lie, then.

Walked aim
less, his pants
off, hard knotty
dick, and hairy
as a rose.

Nobody knows him now.
He's off in the tired sand.

Green flower, like a star,
not a wind to blow it, not a moving
lip of moisture
anywhere. Where are you,
anyassthings, any ass
he windows light that
turns upon the knuckles
day reacting hot hot, then
cold

Go. There's no more love here. Go. Believe
in the gipsies of wordlessness. Down by the seashore.
Ox heart, a cradle the morning sings it, big h, signals

Node

At intervals, the
purest motion
takes my eye.
        Or imagination
rakes across.
        music from my hands
        water running down the drain

what my hands
can
hold
is merely
        beauty.
           these gracious leaves
           the only spleen

waiting to breathe
           or
dying in the bush, the gigantic
rain forests,
           I can not bear to think
           it matters.

Earthshaking: my hand steadies,
when the Fall, October comes,
the garden is a bare footprint
of death.
        It is so easy
        to be made sad.

&
  rattle rattle rattle rattle rattle rattle
  (the devil's blue porsche
    pissing up the road)

Climber of all mounts.
as this paper will turn yellow
& become the thing I answer to.

What interval?
        as this motion
        (these words)
                pass
into

The A, B, C's

For Charles

It rests in me, unmindful

It paces in my chest cavity, not caring

It resists

my probing. It is alert.

It is nameless, as all things

close to us.

You wonder suddenly, as you lope up 20th St.
Why these packhorses of emotion, you cannot
even call to, wild silent nights of
complete despair; Old pack horses,
Why they come here to you, content
in their ancient ugliness, to bite
chunks of Clarke bar from your hands.

Safe now, within the poem, I make my
Indiscreet avowals, my indelicate assumptions
As if this gentle fire that bathed my flesh
was rancor, or fear, or any other of life's idiot progeny.
It is the walls of these words protect me
Throw a fierce cordon
around me, that I may 'signify'
to my heart's content. (My heart's content . . .
What is my heart's content. The mind's content?)

2

It becomes irreversible, an
ellipse (You question my

motives? And you do not even
have a name?) The bridge goes up
so the boats can pass: Sandra is draped
in one of the deck chairs, fondling a
newspaper photograph of me. She is
quite rich, & of course, quite
beautiful. It is part of life's tragedy
that I will never meet her.

                                                3

From the street, across from where
they are tearing down the old church,
you can peer into the windows
of the very poor. The rich have
(more) propriety, and the gorgeous plants
that make shadows
on the ruins.
And everything <u>is</u> ruined for us now. Night
will choke us
if we are out in it.
The largesse of this city
is past. The graciousness
has gone out
of it. Like anything
we are too familiar with.

Only the walls are reluctant
to be put down. Your only
device. The sun rests
among loose bricks
near the base. The heart's
content. The mind is never
maudlin (When Sandra dies
who is it
will love me?)

Because I am standing among the ruins
of ourselves. The sun is still
where we can see it (you know what happens
when it moves . . .) You
cannot even say . . .

                    Or

It is

close to me

and

uncaring. It

stands

in my chest

cavity. It

is unmindful,

& has no name.

I Investigate the Sun

I investigate
the sun. Let it do me
when it come. I am commissioned
by not only charcoal people with brilliant
hues, but laborers in the woods pausing for a moment
to sing while young master dies of that stuff where your blood
too thin to clot. I investigate the sun—and for my trouble, get music
abstract designs I figure out. I fancy myself Pythagoras sometimes, some
times Langston Hughes. You see, I investigate the sun, for people with hard
dirty hands. I find out what its fire and brightness means. For the old lady
polishing floors up on the hill for the permanently smiling, I support her
music, as it trembles against that dazzling flo' I give her Ra or if she want
BB King, I bring that back as well, do tell, I investigate the sun. Call me
agent proxy paid representative, a lobbyist for those without lobbies, think
of me as surrogate for those who sing under impossible weights or resist
　　　[bald
head guys with pointed teeth and white collars pulled outside they coats
suppose to be powerful. My rejoinder and answer, my constant line they all
grow hard against, where are you in the sun's shine, what you know of its
fire? Have you checked your vain insistence against life's life, yellow & red
　　　& atomic before atomic. How does your projection list Ra's ra ra?
No, for real, I investigate the sun. I am paid for this vocation, it's not
above my station, sun checker for a nation, magnifying glass for a class,
　　I investigate the sun. Bring back its dance and music, its design and
hip rime. Sun poet Sun singer Sun warrior Sun why you what you who
　　　[you how you
those my questions as I rise into its hot glamour. I investigate the sun.
Doubt it if you will, what does a shadow know anyway? I investigate
　　　　　　the sun

Courageousness

In the 60's, there was emotion to go around
barreling explosions, at and against, waves
of running, the world itself was feeling, all
feeling. I felt that.
Those shadows haunt us now in various ways.
Women's mouths at odd angles like laughing.
People we know can reappear carrying shadows
which seem to fall from their hands, but musically.
If we wanted to we could locate boxes packed tight
with skulls and odors, murmurs of some distant
hysteria.
There <u>was</u> a rush of us. Some of us wondrous lovely
gorgeous people. That feeling and talking. Such moving
about away and toward. We pointed our fingers alot. We
roared like something out of nature. Like chained beasts
climbing through windows, sometimes we was strange.
The taste of us was acquired and hypnotic, glass crackers
& onions, some dark beer to wash it down. And here these maniac
street lamps are still batting off and on, surely they've had to
change whats inside them making them do that. It cant be the very same

ones. Like these workmen opening our heads
to fix the wires, or put in new batteries,
change a cracked globe or yank the old bulb.
In the 60's there was enough feeling enough emotion
to go round. There was no reason to be square, that's what
we felt. We could do anything, be anything, even free. That's
how young we were. That's now long ago, that was.

Without listing my e.g.'s, elementals of where I thought the shadow of me had passed. Where you been, bend. I could still produce a portrait of lived. Internally they say you feel, an they talkin about the outside of there. Their are the filled up of you seein. Talk it mo. Talk it jo. at you candy sto.

I am the only story telling me here out like this. Telling a seen it living, my breath comes out and the world goes in, your breath and ideas I pick up like picking a banjar.

THE CITY OF NEW ARK

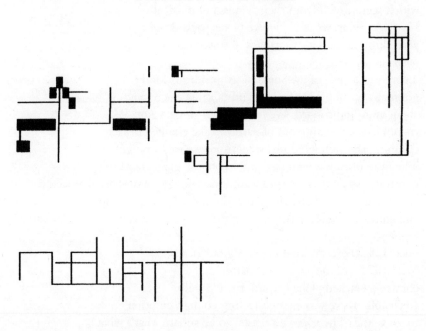

A POEM OF DESTINY
<u>FROM</u> BOOK ONE

***

New Ark Space
is forked
pitch
black Sun
at noon.
The people lay
        roll
        laid &
        stretched yet
            incompletely
                    out!

Yet they are truly <u>out</u>!

Mostly Children
      of the
          Sun

Descendants of the Earth's
      1st Priests
      & Scientists

Try to dig through the concrete
      who 'em is
      & Yes from No

What is Good
      & Why
    The Madness?

*

In New Ark

there's grey
    icicle
Santa Claus
death
bldg.

Lincoln there Fucked up
    in stone.

There's niggers who are completely
    Greasy Heads
    Words Greasy
    Heads inserted
    like pee pee smells
    just behind the
    vestibule

    Yet A Broad
Mother fuckers of all
    descriptions

    gentled by media lighting
the noise holds a framing silence

        Solo
        &
        Ensemble

We all rock w/ the ark
    & try to make our
        33 or 45
        degrees

        Endarkened or
        Dead!

Wit me A
    is repeating

                better to
                        see
              than dream
           better to dream
              than
New Ark   be dead!

is people
borne reborn
in sea
See
Seers
   &
Scene
See in See out
The ark is
      45°
      &
      90°
The 33 must have 12 disciples
      A See
         Sun
         Year
          is
  AFFIRMATIVE

To raise the full
  sail
Like a Pyramid
  The
  Re
  Ra
  Ray
  Rah
  Crown
  Folk
  us
  IG
  NITE
  ARE

(The <u>letter</u>
 The <u>let</u>

  O Ship
      of
  Zion
If we turn
  from thee
  our hearts
  are wither

We are not NEW
  to a
  Knower

  I   PUPIL

 MAGNIFIER

AIR   WATER   EARTH

     FIRE

     SIGN

& SIGNIFIER

PREY & PRAY

     Before life
     & eaten
     by it
     until
We house ourselves
     with
     living
goodness

     SAYS
     SAILS

Intercourse

    Stops
    Latter
    How long
    the raise

the gratitude
    living

    under
        standing
            Can

    Wholly
      &
    Circular

     Go
    Wheel

The Tower
   &
 Trip

 Heaven
   &
 the journey

Tortured Slaves
  below decks
    Chained
     in
    Shit
    &
   Vomit
therein our city
carries in itself
the Move
& the Stop

among the
endless waves
of beings

      Rock Ark
      Role Tied

the things of Standing & Moving
the being & the been

          Black Rhythm
          Turning Blue
              Ra returns
              from his
              Western
              Tour.

New Ark
      Language
      Its words
always
      that show
      the change

      circle
      the square
      the view
      standing
      under
A Pyramid

If you can imagine
  what can be real
if you can find out
What is

That the earth's masters
will save it
& live

the others
will die out

or become
extinct

& unknown.

That we claim the ancient natural
order of humanity
into question

That we are pledged!

    Rapture

Sun blown jism
    perfect
    intelligence

    Go—
    Come
Like The Sun Beats
    Space
    into
    Speech

    Our Hearts
    Rap
The Sun's Language.

       I talked to one "sailor" the other day

What is disappearing is ignorance, wheresom'ever you be in what is ig-
nored. The dross of definition.
We seek what we know, and stumble into error fully armed. We never
thought we'd suffer, never thought pain would get us where it wanted us.
Except when we understood, it was all pain, and we were counting as we
fought, the blows extended by the memory of being everywhere at the

same beat. Except that never is if you try to remember. You are always carried with you, you are never absent, and never alone. People confirm life for us, but they cannot live it for us.

When you begin to see yourself more naturally it is late and the laws weigh against you like a body like a chanting to you a glowing underneath the cloak of name.

We understand how much better the future will be. We are somebody's future, and somebody's past. The present is what we struggle to fully experience and then understand. And it is not waiting for us, its beckoning throbs inside us claiming us yet alive, yet capable of love.

—Interlude Captain

Ark Talks Swims Walks Loves

What ever you're selling, that's out from the jump. No selling. Selling is out, is over. Like the wave, it says goodbye, to all that. What ever you're selling arrest yourself until we get there to speak to you. Our new constitution says No Selling. No Merchants. No Traders. We're for all flavors, and no favors. How could it be a favor, and everything is here to touch. Or speak to. The spirits want no favors, they in flavors. Like the colors. The weather. No favors. NO privilege. And no selling. No selling nothing. NO yourself neither. No selling nothing. You can't give yourself away neither. No free you's and no selling. You is everything, and when that dawns, your day will be here, your ship, o ark, will be and your sea, and your free, oh Ark, o dark lovely ark. Oh place of where, of self of all telling.

So without the merchandising, the commodification, and no favors, or tricks. We depress lies flatter, ground them. So they are merely or merest. So they are brief frowns dispersed by afternoon. Vague woulds and shoulds, keep the do's the be's the is from bad as what is alive hence good. Good is all you got, and that's the truth. That is the living breath, who is breathing is God, that's everything.

The Muslims can tell you if you tell them something, that everything and whatever is left, or right. Every bit of information. Computed Total computed, computing is Allah. Just everything. And its spirit. Its force. It's power. It's history. It's knowledge. Everything! All. A L L.

Now you a something. A some. Sum. What ever. You is. Or who ever. If you don't understand, who you telling it to, then. They a a. AA. AA. They AA. All is A, the 1st principle, the eye, looking down, like the sun rays. God looks down, but that is the sun, like a corpuscle carrying the goods, eats, air, information, anything you gotta have. Prayer needs sun. Preyers, on the other hand, eat, everything, or sell it. They illegal. Prayer is the consultancy with the before yourself, whatever. The not here, which is the majority. The whatever you come out of and will return to. If you can penetrate that veil in some way. Put yr self in touch with the before yourself. The before this world. The after this world. The is that be shoots out of. Pre peter. Pre come. Get in touch with the Not.

****

The coming and going are proofs of the constant is, coming and going back to itself. The science is understanding this and why. We're like animals roaming and biting. But we want more which signifies like my man my ol man on the tree top screaming for a little civilization from the roaring meat eaters checking him out meat frustrated. He telling jokes, throwing doo doo down on 'em. Signifying.

The Africans were the signifying monkey, and still, it seems, must is. Must is, mus aint dont sound right. You got to get back up on the two legs, and signify. You got to do the triple dip jump step and signify. Rap. He in the tree, way high, rapping, beating on the wood. Talking about Hey Hey Hey, I'm what's happening. For half a million years so it was. Then the flood and whatnot. You got weird cousins suddenly. Dudes went off to find out what was and when they return, all ugly, riding horses and shit. We say, damn, what happen my man, you look really weird. Why you look like that? And they growl and start that selling talk. That merchant shit. They ask us do we want to buy something. Nobody know what that mean. Old black John say fuck that buying. He tell em about a picture on a big rock.

They talkin about getting. Nobody understand, except ol John said fuck all that. That's old. You'll get surely fucked up with that. Took all the jewelry and shit with em. Some ol plates, went away from here talking the same shit. Buying and Selling. Last dumb shit they say is that stealing

is where it's really at. Talk about stealing is high art. Fuck it, we went
back up and looked at the 1st sea, the 1st cloud, the 1st voice, the first
song, and felt cool. For centuries.

Yours,
"Ark Am" 8/89

Ark

Wants to know
Wants to be and is for that
Wants not to
  afloat, air driven, love driven, growing into the babe
  seed is what you saw, story is what "your" stored of that
  so the seed carries all the information, of scene, an re
  makes whatever to be.
Ark lives to live. Life is specific not abstract, not an IOU,
except seeing means you seen, and the scene goes on as you do as
you are as you will, want, to be, you keep lying to yrself, but
when God is busted, watch who be in the papers. God exists only
as the total of what is
Goodness is God
's only life
life is God
Death is not evil, Death is the beginning of the new year. Yeah!
Only what cannot exist is evil. That's why.

Murder is the illusion that life is evil. So that is evil. Sin
is what does not exist. Sin means without. With Out being the
never. The not is not the never. The never cannot. The not, is
what's womb.

Dont you ever get tired of animals and living
with animals in a cage? Dont you get tired
of animals telling you how humans live? Dont you ever get tired
    [of the Dead,
messing you up and they on vacation?

At the top of the highest building is where the new is. The
known is below already what is not, the new is in its womb
waiting to be fertilized. The fertilizer brain. Your story is
your tail, your snake mind, ideas are the day time for the sun,
of the black woman. Night. Who is is. An Ethiopian.

Everything is a real idea, the life before the idea, the womb of
the idea is real thing, the idea is the path into and away from
the real, is, carries every, idea is thing breathing, seeds. The
G is a seed, A, 1st principle, B, from the is, C existence, in
the sea, where the seeds are, see hence seen.

    D is the specific where, that manifesting of. E the out of,
the energy, what issues, what goes, exhaust, ex it, from which
the it breath issues. Blood always talk precise. D shit aint
right he say.

    Like a cry, E, EEEEE, the issue, the going, the gone. The F
is the flag, the being, the signal of, proof of, existence of.
Speed it means, because that determines appearance, how fast
among fast, to mean where. The G, is the seed. G! Also gravity
measurement, what force into is the substance. Earth and Sun
mixed with water, H the tower, the prayer for consolidating
building, development. So I, is the God number 9, the eye of Ra.
Sun and Life, derived therefrom.

    The 10 is the rebeginning. I re turned, like the circle,
and we arcs of carried in its being, as ourselves, eggs to egos.
The egg entering the cycle of be is ego, the egg, is stored
information. What I seed!

    Ra is Re, because only that is can re produce!

****

    Actually, 1 is 2. I got that from Monk 1st, then Marx! 0 is
1! The whole is Un. Unitary. Atone means to get it together!
Be one. 1 requires 2 elements. The is (0 = All) and the being.
Their connection, via "night's" history, her tail, memory,
absolute everywhere&thing. A tail, A joint. Connect. Jazz is
the meeting the motion the heat the feeling the coming, is being
Re being. Be is always Blue when it first get here.

"Fucking" on the other hand means beating, as in fighting!
Not love. The "other" beating, rhythm, as in Be At ing, self
conscious reflection of everything. Life conscious of Life. Its
perfection is its ultimate turn, goal ("gold").

We move supposedly from Fucking To Love As Animals to Humans
to Self Created Consciousness, as total harmonic expressions of
the endlessly expressed.

Be is is and however and wherever from is manifest
specifically. All is All is. Is Is.
The conflict of the journey away from the Mother is summed
up as Fucked Up for the totally negative vs Pregnant and the
ecstasy of Creation. As Art. (Exists as opposed to Not). Vs
Arent. Art Vs. Arent! The Creative Principle Vs The Death
Principle.
The Devil then wants Never. Wants Arent. The Devil is not
Mythology, there is a scientific principle this concept
expresses. Religion was literally The Way of The Sun, The Way of
Life.
The Sun Worshippers confirm the obvious, the most
significant explanation of how and why we are here and everything
else we see. No Sun No thing. We get jumpy when it goes on
tour, not to mention goes out forever? Ha!

Mythology and Metaphysics are the lies the sins the tools of
Devils what pushes evil De Evil as it is Death. It is a lie
since it is impossible to dismiss the be and even lies must
pretend to be the truth. Must pretend to be real, and their
realness attests to the constancy of is, as definer and
continuer. We test our understanding, like we breathe, in and
out. The spirit, literally breath, the top of the church, the
spires, the spiral, like the dialectical motion of is, the
infinity sign turned upright like it sposed to be, not parallel,
the endless mindless metal frenzy. Cat nip. Bees get high on
hot honey.
But turning and rising, the spirit. The advance to what we
were always. The animal is the distance the out breathing away
from and at the same time, essence, to rebecome its total and by
doing be whatever it is then expressing or there expressing . . .

its where (wear) tale (tail) time is the reverse expression of
expression. Emit is powerful, the explanation of time, slow
motion. What stops is evil because it is a lie. An illusion.
Time expresses elapse, or power, or distance, or history, the
number of seeds, except if there was such a real thing as time,
there could be no is.

Time will become obsolete when the snapshots of everything
and everything are conscious love.

So we are life fighters. Fighting for life. Death is our
enemy. Ignorance and Disease, its weapons. Consciousness is our
God self, the everything else goes and comes but the path, the
road, the you we love, the me we need, is alive. Be for life and
against its enemies. This is one things I learn.

Marxism simply tries to bring the Divine (Mystery) into our
fingers as known and usable. As it is. As long as there are
mysteries we are animals. And our animal spirit is what kills us.

****

In Ark everybody know we need love
tell by the way they walk
tell by the way they talk
by the way they dress, what they love
what they hate

Everybody in the Ark   know
We need love.

This is where Freedom come in.

Blue Monk!

****

JODI BRAXTON

Conversion

I

early   mist
bring back the dawn
i
follow flock

reach blues ancestor
astral bird
startling grace of white
flapping strangely slow
like spirits   ride
into   streaked morning
cirrus and sunrise   arching
night's baptismal blackness

hands   tear   wet
rushes   briars   blood
my heart beat over
the siren

wing/wail

II

i did not
hear myself scream

pulp of nausea
woman of lips that tremble
hair full of mud

bed slept clothes and wash night purple love
come glide to the swamp

i the woman nude with serpents
and a saucy rhythm to guide love

come pain surrender blackness
humming stomach wretch
spiral falling bird

i woke in the mud wet
sound battered body
hands rust red patches drying

a water mocassin on either side
to guide me through the swamp

there is pain
but it is not like other pain

i am not afraid
i am not afraid when snakes drop down out of trees
to twine with womanflesh
arms   breasts   thighs

through smoke
see the spirit

birds again
of a broken wing
fallen and burned
where snakes led me

to fall from such a height
nobody singing   nobody singing
down the lean black chute
out of night into the heat of the day

the wail of the love of the wail
                         had ceased

III

whips
i crack the mocassins from around my legs
and lean back dancing
laughing in the flames

in the fire hot ashes there
i found a baby bird
a wet envelope of skin

and i make me a nest in the woods for my charge
a nest in the wilderness lined with hair
from the nape of my neck

i pluck worms from the sod and
serpents from the field

i kill field mice with my hands
to nourish the phoenix

this is why i came
into the marsh/ to forget
men women houses pain

to burn my clothes
and make me a cover
of snakeskin and prayer

an altar in the wood

HAROLD CARRINGTON

Lament

while my city gently sleeps
the lonely moan a weary blues
reflecting
on the poet's silent, unobserved departure,
contemplating
the poet shoes he left behind
& are as yet
unfilled—

Ray
now I feel like Nellie Lutcher
want to sing and fornicate,
make swinging Jersey City
meet the family
friends
& Grace,
go over to some convenient village
pad
dig the cool—controversal
Brubeck beams,
(man, don't be a drag)
investigate
the cause of bitte Barbara's
motavation,
maybe chase a few Lolitas
in Central Park
on the way up to Harlem
to have a ball,
(funky)
cultivate a wine habit
so I can comprehend
& shout

THUNDERBIRD SUITE,
split to the far coast
blow in the cellar,
down to Mexico for bull fights
mushrooms
& crazy visions,
then in a blaze of violence
we'll quit-it out the back door
on some crowded city street
coming to a screeching
halt—

while my city gently sleeps
this lonely moans a weary blues
reflecting
on the poet's silent, unobserved departure,
contemplating
the poet shoes he left behind
& are as yet
unfilled . . .

Woo's People

SOME ANTI-
BLASPHEMY
OR LARK

(DENIAL)

CHALLENGE
TO THE CHALLANG-
ABLE

(DENIAL)

CUNNING FANGS
OF
AGE

(DE____?)

O
SWEET & VIRGINED
MOTHER . . .

sting—
a south carolina
ave.
folk tale

squating
in front of perry's stick hall
in hustling clothes:
20 dollar panama,
long shoes
& short sleeve summer sportshirt
(open down the front
for an envious glance
at scotch plaid
underwear)
the fabulous wine—
last of the red-hot mackmen,
with the everpresent jug
five star half & half
(the ice action)
stashed
inconspicuously, momentarily safe
from the garbage can dancers of every set.
& laying
for any down with it
can't quit it
stud
who'll take the wooden nickle.

STEPHEN CHAMBERS

Her

... A—JA—BU;
                 A—JA—BU
                        (bu—su)
                                  sue / san
                 I—Kemo—San
      Ja—A—Bu
                  Ja—A—Bu
                      i / kemo / no / san
                 San / (frisco???)
Bu—A—Ja
      (jabua)
              A-JA-BU
                        ... "her" ...

JAYNE CORTEZ

Drying Spit Blues

Tonight the whooping moan of invading blues
    with its clef of troubled hearts
with its double stomp burn of woman flesh
    spitting with the whirlwind of spitting cobras
spitting with the meaning of Anna Nzinga
    flashflooding blues
of great blues migrations
    the great blues of howling sudan
great blues in a conflict of nubian throbs
    among the faces chiseled from memphis
among the cataracts spitting from ethiopia
    the great blues of drying spit
with its escalator of razors
    forefinger of pistol whips
quadrangle of knuckle bones
    basin of fish hooks
equator salt
    the whooping taste of invading blues
of broken whistles
    radiated fox holes
a grenade of camel hair
    calypso of neckscars
old blues
    intravenous blues
blues with a procession of blows
     the blows in the mouth of the goatheads of death
a commemoration to famine
    right up to our chests
afterskulls of invading blues
    of bombed out groans
150 rockets between screams
    meat hooks smelling into smells of needle-tracked ribs

dead crows   fried feathers   spoiled calamares
    and eyes of sculpted slugs
and silver ants on lower lids painted charcoal
and long teeth in amber jels
    and tongue flaming tongue of sweetheart rings
of ruby snakes with veins of irridescent smoke studs
    a squadron of lips made of cucka burrs
    a salty dirge of sapless pinchers
a mirage of pulsing green roosters
secret dogs
polychrome spirits
    head-quart of bullface throat slitters
right up to our chins
    sparkling without lizard juice
mutilations without mucous
    a concave of widowfish entering flies
a circle of jackals cocked on the moon
    a cylinder sun without holes
and once again warships rush to other ports
and once again relief is too late
and once again a shriveling solution
    the code name for buzzards
wrist-bones on altar of another jaw
    illuminations
right up to our nostrils
in howling sudan
    in nubian throbs
in faces chiseled from memphis
    the shrinking shrines of whooping flesh
of invading skeletons
    of spreading saharas
of drying spit
    tonights Blues

Under the Edge of February

Under the edge of February
in hawk of a throat
hidden by ravines of sweet oil
by temples of switch blades
beautiful in its sound of fertility
beautiful in its turban of funeral crepe
beautiful in its camouflage of grief
in its solitude of bruises
in its arson of alert

Who will enter its beautiful calligraphy of blood

Its beautiful mask of fish net
mask of hubcaps mask of ice picks mask
of watermelon rinds mask of umbilical cords
changing into mask of rubber bands
Who will enter this beautiful mask of
punctured bladders moving with a mask of chapsticks

Compound of Hearts   Compound of Hearts

Where is the lucky number for this shy love
this top-heavy beauty bathed with charcoal water
self-conscious against a mosaic of broken bottles
broken locks   broken pipes   broken
bloods of broken spirits broken through like
broken promises

Landlords   Junkies   Thieves
enthroning themselves in you
they burn up couches they burn down houses
and infuse themselves against memory
every thought
a pavement of old belts

every performance
a ceremonial pickup
how many more orphans   how many neglected shrines
how many stolen feet   stolen gums
stolen watchbands of death
in you how many times

Harlem

hidden by ravines of sweet oil
by temples of switch blades
beautiful in your sound of fertility
beautiful in your turban of funeral crepe
beautiful in your camouflage of grief
in your solitude of bruises in
your arson of alert
beautiful

Phraseology

I say things to myself
in a bitch of a syllable
an off tone wisp remarkable
in weight and size
completely savage to the passing of silence
through mass combinations of moisture
uncaked in pockets of endless phraseology
moving toward sacred razors
like air   like untangled bush
over a piece of dead scar
instant in another smashed ear lobe
shivering between word echoes of
word shadows
jugular veins of popular contradictions
well dressed and groomed in the mirror of language
transparent and useless against
the impulsive foam
of a spastic

Indelible

Listen i have   a complaint to make
my lips are covered
with thumb prints
insomnia sips me
the volume of isolation
is up to my thyroid
and i won't disappear
can you help me

Opening Act

To be the opening act
and absorb all slobber
all praises
all stares
all insults in a rhythm tube of
fallopian teeth

To be the opening act
and not forget the odor of roaches
in a diamond miner's eyeball
flame of a dead flint
listen to this suspect number one
because to be the opening act
and plant feet in asses of corrupt politicians
without a time clock without correct wages
without profits without bitterness
without a breeding place for pain
is a bitch
so pass the word around

To be the opening act
and know when to duck when to salute
when to cover up
when to fight
when to scream when to dive into your solitude
and detoxify whistles in your kidneys
salt dry curses in your eardrums
and then laugh into the drunken gallbladders of the night
you have to be rich in blood vessels to
bury that act in someone's mouth at 3 am every morning
so don't fuck with me
I want to be the opening act between this planet and the sun
in health   in sickness   in death
I said primp on your own time baby

because I'm walking the entire motion of space
in rawflesh of this opening act to end all acts
and I don't have to impose myself on anybody
so throw your wig into the ocean
I know I'm the opening act of acts here
because all of a sudden
someone blew smoke in my face and yelled boooo

Into This Time

For Charles Mingus

Into this time
of steel feathers blowing from hearts
into this turquoise flame time in the mouth
into this sonic boom time in the conch
into this musty stone-fly time sinking into
the melancholy buttocks of dawn
sinking into lacerated whelps
into gun holsters
into breast bones
into a manganese field of uranium nozzles
into a nuclear tube full of drunk rodents
into the massive vein of one interval
into one moment's hair plucked down into
the timeless droning fixed into
long pauses
fixed into a lash a ninety-eight minutes screeching into
the internal heat of an ice ball melting time into
a configuration of commas on strike
into a work force armed with a calendar of green wings
into a collection of nerves
into magnetic mucus
into water pus of a silver volcano
into the black granite face of Morelos
into the pigeon toed dance of Mingus
into a refuge of air bubbles
into a cylinder of snake whistles
into clusters of slow spiders
into spade fish skulls
into rosin coated shadows of women wrapped in live iguanas
into coins into crosses into St. Martin De Porres
into the pain of this place changing pitches beneath
fingers swelling into

night shouts
into day trembles
into month of precious blood flowing into
this fiesta of sadness year
into this city of eternal spring
into this solo
on the road of young bulls
on the street of lost children
on the avenue of dead warriors
on the frisky horse tail fuzz zooming
into ears of every madman
stomping into every new composition
everyday of the blues
penetrating into this time

This time of loose strings in low tones
pulling boulders of Olmec heads into the sun
into tight wires uncoiling from body of a strip teaser on the table
into half-tones wailing between snap and click
of two castanets smoking into
scales jumping from tips of sacrificial flints
into frogs yodeling across grieving cults
yodeling up into word stuffed smell of flamingo stew
into wind packed fuel of howling dog throats slit into
this January flare of aluminum dust falling into
laminated stomach of a bass violin rubbed into red ashes
rubbed into the time sequence of
this time of salmonella leaking from eyeballs of a pope
into this lavender vomit time in the chest into
this time plummage of dried bats in the brain into
this wallowing time weed of invisible wakes on cassettes into
this off-beat time syncopation in a leopard skin suit
into this radiated protrusion of time in the desert into
this frozen cheek time flying with the rotten bottoms of used tuxedos
into this purple   brown   grey   gold minus zero time trilling into
a lime stone crusted Yucatan belching
into fifty six medallions shaking
into armadillo drums thumping
into tambourines of fetishes rattling
into an oil slick of poverty symbols flapping

into flat-footed shuffle of two birds advancing
into back spine of luminous impulses tumbling
into metronomes of colossal lips ticking
into a double zigzag of callouses splitting
into foam of electric snow flashing into this time
of steel feathers blowing from hearts
into this turquoise flame time in the mouth into
the sonic boom time in the conch
into this musty stone fly time sinking into
the melancholy buttocks of dawn

LAWRENCE S. CUMBERBATCH

I Swear to You, That Ship Never Sunk in Middle-Passage!

Tugging at containment
     all yields for the sake of bursting feet
         scuffling in the furrowed yesterdays

Inn beyond "the man's" whirl,
     funky dark as the hovel,

us children never sink
dancing on the water of futility

Never,

         never

Tomorrow is for the planters.

Plantation people dance at the Harlem Inn, Winstonville, Mississippi.

Again the Summoning

in new romance with blackness
burst the thread of last words
off the tangled spool
      where glare
      too many pictured kingdoms
painting bullets a missile
      girdled by noble goals
the heroic fabric of soulful minds
weaves thru
         imagined jungles
to a boogaloo party
of rainbow chiefs
      where beauty whimpers of exhaustion
      and the melody soon ends.

In the Early Morning Breeze

In the early crystal morning
   of glass-shattered streets
where the breeze has no challenge
   to weathered breasts
as of bahing sheep
gingerly as the leaf
     fall a thousand times
never to ground
I to no line
    remember ethiopia
   clothed in her tattered lion's cloth
of popes' and bishops'
and longshoremen's kisses
     wispily sailing
from deep-water departure piers.

RUDY BEE GRAHAM

A LYNCHING   FOR SKIP
JAMES

. . . they may get better
but they will never be well . . .
We know
     the dying
     a museum death
     the funeral homes
     of no rhythm
     in the music
     no breathing
     on the canvasses
we have seen
the unseeing steel
blue eyes on the rockets
the money-green gazes
from the subways

flag uniforms on parochial
killers wiping us out

from the kitchens we have felt
the cold seeping from the pale
shadows they make
along the walls
(as economic as death)

from classrooms on the streets
we have heard the silence
of their words calling us
out of life to their Snowdom
in grave-school-yards we have known them

using Time as a weapon
defending deaths they have coffined
in color tones and sentences

We have danced in the tree-grey static
of their glances
and they have stolen us
into their catacombs
cleaning up

You sang to me of the trenches
in your eyes the humanless years
have wrenched you through
and yet too wise for bitterness you
sound more like a human
than anyone

And I would murder the walking
shrouds that have hammered the cry
in your throat with their too deep
an ignorance of unfeeling ears
        they cannot feel
        they have no soul
and you have made your misery
music they have not heard
they cannot hear
        the humanity
        in the chords
        of the whines
        in the moans
    they cannot hear
And I would electrocute
the phantoms who slit
warm throats with stainless steel
eyes looking away
to pluto
And I would gas the ghosts
who strangle us with mercantile facts
and neckties of a futile civilization

We are the children of Carthage
and we are singing
the only songs

in our blood
the only prophecies
of man kind to come

and from the kitchens we can see
    god with his
    broken neck
    hanging
    from the
    moon
    that waits
    over the western road
    like a gangrene
    destination

    And sometimes
    the soul-fingered cloud
    in your voice
    closes his deathray eyes
    and cuts him down

Without Shadow

death in so many
forms (supple, unsupple)
a difference
of footprints
and clothing

the economic classes
of death
in the morning
making rain
last on the skin
of slum
children

a dying out
of windows
part of the body
           eyes.
in the street
loitering
a head
to be picked up
by any body open
without curtain

a man
waiting for himself
to take away
the blind.

but otherwise
in my time
nothing memorable
no soul.

but we are so beautiful sometimes my skeleton
melts from my body like a cry
losing sound
and limp I think myself no further.
the end of a pause. a death
into something somewhere else beginning

after us.

(wanting to stretch a bridge
that doesn't have the strength.
so much waiting in that sometimes
we so beautiful

an evening leaf on spider silk
dangling   from the moon
in someone's eyes
a second
strangles you to them
you cannot move
and limp you let it pass
and you forget)

remembering
we are the bridge
I climb to the top
of myself looking down
at the green
black blood biting the girders
of ages cannot hold
an afterthought
for long

the bridge
a nobles non-alternative
for the dying.

I am thirteen again
waiting for my sperm
somehow wise

with the grey-eyed wisdom of
my death affair with Time
I shall not follow

our children will only come
upon themselves
without us.
silent the way
light through glass
without shadow.

WILLIAM J. HARRIS

A Grandfather Poem

A grandfather poem
must use words of great dignity.

It can not
contain words like:
Ubangi
rolling pin
popsicle,

but words like:
Supreme Court
graceful
wise.

Practical Concerns

From a distance, I watch
a man digging a hole with a machine.
I go closer.
The hole is deep and narrow.
At the bottom is a bird.

I ask the ditchdigger if I may climb down
and ask the bird a question.
He says, why sure.

It's nice and cool in the ditch.
The bird and I talk about singing.
Very little about technique.

DE LEON HARRISON

A Collage for Richard Davis—Two Short Forms

Form I

Valley Floors

                        trickling
some god cursed   to spew   slimy
                                                  mouthed
four curdling   streams   flowing   intrinsically
fast fingers
(phantom digits)
snowy pines   frozen ponds   stocking caps
laughing-moaning   building-streaking   slashing
pricking   distorting
autumn winds   browns   reds   yellows
pizzicato lines   double stopping   expiring
strumming quietly

Form II

(silence)

Formula for Blue Blues Babies

Babies born blue
Soil tilled
    cultivated
to host thrill giving
Poppies
That will help them later
to overcome
If my contemporaries don't
Get there first

Yellow

birds & sunlight
a piece for *bird calls* , *bells*   apprx. Time 3 min.
          & silence

bells should be light tinkle or chime like to
medium ring

varied improvisational rest

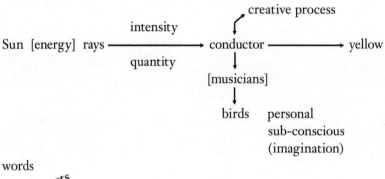

words
    3 poets

DAVID HENDERSON

Downtown-Boy Uptown

For Mary Williams

Downtown-boy uptown
Affecting complicity of a Ghetto
and a sub-renascent culture.
Uptown-boy uptown for graces loomed to love.

Long have I walked these de-eternal streets
Seeking a suffice or a number to start my count.
Cat-Walk
Grotesque Pelican manger
Trampling Trapezium to tapering hourglass
Behind the melting sun.

I love a girl then.
My 140th St. gait varied from my downtown one.
I changed my speed and form for lack of a better tongue.
Then was, love you, Pudgy:
Thin young woman with a fat black name.
It is the nature of our paradox that has us
Look to the wrong convex.

II
I stand in my low east window looking down.
Am I in the wrong slum?
The sky appears the same;
Birds fly, planes fly, clouds puff, days ago . . .
I stand in my window.
Can I ride from my de-eternal genesis?
Does my Exit defy concentric fish-womb?
Pudgy: your Mama always said Black man
Must stay in his own balancing cup.

Roach on kneebone I always agreed.
Was this Black man's smile enjoying guilt
Like ofay?

Long has it been that I've mirrored
My entrances through silk screen.

III
Did this Tragedian kiss you in anticipation
Of blood-gush separating from your black mirror?
Did I, in my complicity-grope relay the love
Of a long gone epoch?

    sometimes questions are not questions
If I desire to thrust once more, If I scamper to embrace
Our tragedy in my oblique arms! . . . .

                                       Nevermind.
You know.
You are not stupid, Pudgy.
You look for nothing of a Sun where you live,
Hourglass is intrinsic . . . where you live.
The regeneration in your womb is not of my body.
You have started your count
I cannot.

Sketches of Harlem

To Langston Hughes

It was Tiny's habit
to go down to THE GREAT WHITE WAY
without understanding the subway ride.

In the Harlem morning
when sirens remind you
that you're burning—

Tiny Habit
Handy's broad
Hi-Hat Lounge 7th Avenue
in the morning rabbit
refuse mildew
with Negro for a color
and nothing for a hue.

In Williams

in williams
i would drink all 1100 springs of texas
by way of the pearl beer company

in *le quartier*
williams down n dirty bar & grill
chickens dance on concrete floors
as the sparrow flies Friday night
jaz n dixie regal & falstaff lager
local beer demons fix black lips

twin partners spar
yogi trousers bend the knees
inside that other body
shirttails fly in moon winds
charity hospital chloroform wall paper
glows   fire & water talisman
                                         (Are you eligible?)

crescent city beelzebub horns
guide prowl cars below sea level
thru gulf of mexico nights

off bourbon street
the jass musicians are preserved
in a hall
old granddad stands sentry
in alabaster /

en la calle burgundy
black scarecrows surrender
when the light of tony's superette / fails

piccolo say
thread the needle
we gonna do it

cat tails bump n grind
puppet pelvis strings
belly rein
high in hand
this i can do
that i cannot
the elderly gentleman laughs
all the pictures off the wall /

razors in the wind
thread the needle
thread the needle
we gonna do it

Lock City

in a collection of sun
lost in the street
east or west
sharp as black & white
layers of light
upon shade
                              lost in the streaks
as the wind runs horizontal water cycles
the city is so bright
everything seen
shadows dance
mad fall coats   scenery on rollers
on amber st. marks place
the tenuous line between eye and medulla
                              east nor west

Blackman in the Desecrated Synagogue—Living in the Last Days

Smoke reminds me of mother. She would say those who smell of
smoke are poor. It hangs me up. When we go out we will smell like
smoke and look like soot.

Piero Helizger

In candy kitchens   so many days
Watching fire. Elemental déjà vu. Scenes of symbolic
loft aloft. Visions like fire writhe. Too many memories
jibes with the rhythm of the blues. My background is
played on the radio twenty-four hours a day. The tunes.
The place. The space.
The tables the pipes the battles the odors the pipes and
yes the boo. All in re-embrace. Rembrace. Time of winning
who I left yesterday. Achievement symbolic waste of tired
men toiling over graveyard of indestructible bones.
Fireplace burns wood. Fire burns fast and slow—its—speed indecipherable.
Spires sparkle. Pops smoke and soot.
Of eternity lost tribes sitting afore fires looking into
the future. Past cognizance of selfsame event. Elemental
medium symbiosis fulcrum catalyst. Means light and heat
fire and water. Days rooms nights blaze tables pipes.

CALVIN HERNTON

Being Exit in the World

Being exit in the world
Is all over my hands
In my mouth, hair
Like syrup
Being absurd in the world sticks between
My fingers, and webs them.

Man cycled and ethos lorned
Exit in the hole alone I defend it,
I make it come alive, I come alive, explode.
I fill it with my substance, my finger, tongue,
Tears, anything.

Void in the world I exist.
All the crevices of life are meat tight
With the heat of my sweat,
I abandon none; yet abandoned am I
Alienated as at first sea eye keys unlocked
Fish hook from earth worm.
I am every project I fill, every mouth of food
Is my being in every body;
And being exits me, rots root and tree top,
My essence visits a million dark rooms

Pulsing, I lie naked with sleepers;
I choose them into being—
It is my ecstasy,
I am the leper who suffers to be.

The Wall

Wall
They were driven everywhere
And always from there were ghosts

She said stroke the tiger's bladder
Wait until April rolls down that river
And sing Where O Where O

Whispering in darkness they say
The wall crumble into broken clocks
The un-make-up mind continued making speeches

She said sweetheart I love that naked desperado
Where O Where O

Wall!
And they were driven everywhere

Medicine Man

North of Dark
North from Shango
In kangaroo jungle of West Lost
Dressed in hide of fox
Dressed at last to kill
Thirteen grains of sand
Seven memories
And Ten voices whispering in a rock

Time medicine riddle
Time rock disguised in evil bite
In devil flight
Time encloses cycles
Voice memory
Revolve
Age leaps upon the lips
Hawk! Kiss of hatred
Is turtle blood
Is love's hair buried in an old tin can

Then I said to my knee bones
Teach me how to bend
My knee bones hardening seven memories
Recalled what I fail to know
In an estranged familiar tongue
Said:
          If you must go
          Go by the abandoned railroad yard

The muddy ditch
The lizard infested by-pass
Flank to the left where an old black woman
With prayers for you in her wrinkled hands

Cupped in an old-fashioned apron lap
Rocks eternally
Eternal rock
Rocking chair
Pause, leave a tear
Beneath the fallen viaduct
But do not linger
For the dead rock is never
Home is never where you were born

Oh Grandmother, figurine gris gris Goddess
Do I
Should I
Can I live so that I may die easily

Thirty years wrinkle
My belly folds
When I sit
When I stand
My belly spreads

Thirty years contending with Satan
The backbones breaking pain
Thirty times ten removed from gods
My fathers knew

Oh, Shango, man of mothers
Will you join us in trance
In eating the bowels of black man
Who is our victim
Who no longer is father of his man

And do I approve
If I do not approve
I have done somebody wrong
If I do approve
Why should I approve
Thirty times ten removed from voices
Ancestral

Birth is April fish belly.
Love is love going the wrong way.
And if I weep
I weep for my twin rising out of
The marriage womb leaping upon me mid-years

Hence I put away old handed-down ailments
Put away hence common motives that drive men
To conventional madness
And weep for the mother of my twin
And conjure Dance on pages of medicine book
    of white hands
And by ceaseless slapping on genital organ
And by eating of embryos taken from ovaries
    of the dead infant boy
Leaping to meet me death
If I weep at all

We may not live until love
Until moon
And if I approve
Eating entrails of multitude of living victims
It will not resurrect those already dead
It will not heal ear and tongue of betrayal
April is a time of betrayal
And I do not approve
I do not approve

And if I pray
I pray not to God or Shango
I pray to bellies of deep sea sharks
And pray for us survived west lost
North of dark in chains

After the present pain is gone.
The hate who roars in the brain.
The one who sucks my breath like an evil cigarette
The one who crushes the young men and smashes them
Who will be left to care

So shameless black men speak blood of their sisters!
And will it if I weep
Drive away juju of the fox
And if I pray
I have done somebody wrong

And if I do not pray
I pray for those who will live until moon
And to those residing in evil bite
And to the old black woman living in my wounds
And for the twin of the father who falters

I pray because I was born
And have sinned my birth to clay.

Wherefore I said to my knee bones
Instruct me in how to stand
Teach me how to love and how to die
And my bones wherein the hot oil
Of the sun is contained
Said:
      Go by the abandoned railroad yard
      Flank to the left your black mamma
      Is rocking
      Seven memories recall what
      You know
      North of the dark path in juju jungle
      Age leaps upon the lips and caresses
      The kiss of wisdom is love
      Hold thirteen grains of sand
      Look at the sun until it three-times
      Blinds you, and listen
      Listen to ten voices
      Singing in that rocking chair

      Singing in that rock!
      Singing in that rock!

JOSEPH JARMAN

what we <u>all</u>
would have of
each other
the men of
the sides of ourworlds
contained
in a window
      yes"go contrary
        go sing   "
to give
all you have
yourself
to each yourself
yet never
to remember
        to look back
into a void
—it is time
yes; to move from
yourself to
yourself again
to know

what you are

song

I

Non-cognitive aspects of the City
where Roy J's prophecies become
the causes of children

once quiet black blocks of stone
encasements/of regularity

sweet now
intellectual dada
of vain landscapes
the city

long history
upheaval
the heath valueless in its norm
now/gravestone or gingercakes
the frail feel of winter's wanting
crying to leaves they wander
seeing the capital vision
dada
new word out of the twenties of chaos
returned in the suntan jar
fruits of education/with others

non-cognitive — these motions
embracing sidewalk heroes
the city   each his own
where no one is more alone than any other
moan, it's the hip plea for see me, see me, i exist
exit the tenderness for power/black or white
no difference now/the power/city

II

Could   have spirits   among   stones
uppity   the   force   of   becoming
what   art   was   made   to   return

the   vainness   of   our   pipes,   smoking
near   fountains,   the   church   pronouncing
the   hell/   of   where   we   are

Could have spirits among stones
uppity the force of becoming
what art was made to return
the vainness of our pipes, smoking
near fountains, the church pronouncing
the hell/of where we are

couldhavespiritsamongstonesuppitytheforceof
becomingwhatartwasmadetoreturnthevainnessof
ourpipes,smokingnearfountains,thechurchpro
nouncing
<u>the hell</u>
of where we are

III

quiet city
wanting each to stop the/pain
it must be done — expresso
old fashioned sheet about boy thighs
war—their homeliness
common tools
the knife and gun
castration in store
the tarred spotlight against
what hope we have

non-cognitive
these elements of how
no more

shall it be better
the passion of other saints
ungodly
shall poison drinking hoodlum talk

to describe the callousness
of these penny fares
among/my friends they say they are
the hair torches
eggs for these deaths
internal zones of where they go
where they—come from
(in the language of the street)
internal
these states on planes
farout as what these lives become
thoughts
final last work there
spots for treason
last word
non-cognitive
doom

TED JOANS

The Overloaded Horse

On a battu le cheval, au mois de Mai and they ate him
his buttons were crushed into powder for their soup
   his hair was wovened into ship sails
his foreskin was sewn by an antique dealer
his manure supplied several generations with xmas gifts
   and now they speak bad of him, the horse, the head of their family
   On a battu le cheval, au mois de Mai and they ate him
   his earwax was packaged in America
his rump was displayed on early morning garbage trucks
   his crossed eye is on loan to a soap museum
   his manners have since been copied by millions of glass blowers
   and still yet, they spit at his stable, the horse, the head of the house
   On a battu le cheval, au mois de Mai and they ate him .
his ribs were riveted outside an airbase
his knees bend in shadows of Russia
   his shoelaces are used to hang lovely violinists
his dignity is exported as a dairy product to the Orient
   and in spite of it all, those he loved most, lie and cheat horse's heirs
   On a battu le cheval, au mois de Mai and they ate him
   his tears now drown the frowning yachtsmen
his urine flows rapidly across millionaires estates
his annual vomit destroys twelve dictator's promises a year
his teeth tear wide holes in the scissor maker's Swiss bank account
   and even in death, filled with revenge, they eat him, again and again
  they deny   and lie as they speak bad of the horse, the head of their
house, the father of their home

PERCY JOHNSTON

Round About Midnight, Opus #6

Night descends while
The coal-oil driven wind
Taxis with six-pod force
Past orange and white chessboard
Sheds, past cargo scales
In mudwalls which have the
Stillness of chockwheel monoplanes.
I rest on a concrete apron
In onyx night,
'Round about midnight, with
Navigation lamps inactive.
Sleep, with the force of
Twenty-four thousand thrusted
Pounds, arrived unburnished,
But the gas turbine wind
Reduces our plexiglass blisters
To polyethelene lumps
Chilling chockwheel, monoplane me.
Dawn flies the holding pattern,
Waiting for the tower's wink.
Dawn kisses the runway,
Decelerating into morning.

Lexington Avenue Express

As I sit squeezing lemon juice on dacron shirt, beside
Sunglassed brown conductor who straws the final bottle of pop
Suspended above a Yonkers Raceway omnibus, facing
The patriarch of every jukebox, who contains
A size twelve cola model, I
Become the Lexington Avenue Express; I walk through
Myself even as I stop at every local station from
Woodlawn to 125th, I even stop at 86th, I bounce along
bantam-like on superway vaulting the Bronx.

I walk through myself, forgetting
How many faded numbers I am, forgetting
How many dull black fans I am, forgetting
How many tons of copper
Wire I am at home with, until I
Leave my unself and locomote my real
Self, and in disbelief, I am outside
My two selves until I discover terra
Incognita at Burnside station.

Oh points of alternating incandescent thrill!
Oh pin-prick rows of white contentment, and
Filtered triplets, filtered spraylettes of full
Chorused amber! Oh catatonic reds and intermittent
Flashes of blue! We're roaring by 103d street girders
Through a sacred concrete catacomb, through the barrel
Arch vault while my brakes moan on Sparrows Point
Fabricated rails from ambivalent strains of my
Preternatural movements which couple my several selves.

We're at Grand Central, time for all of us to leave me.
What did you expect for a lousy token—love!—or love?

to paul robeson, opus no. 3

I

A. N. Marquis has erased
Your song, your Raritan relatives
Sneer. Your brothers
Fire 24 point boldface projectiles, saluting
Felons—and forget your song.

They've forgot the chorus
Of your hymn which memorialized
Oriental urban renewal;
They've forgot your song
Which stood Brooklyn on its feet
Certain technicolor leaf
Saturday afternoons.

The new song's sung
By maintenance men
Who unplug coinchangers,
Who unscramble binary code;
By your brothers who have the
Prime trinitarian person on
Auction block,
Airconditioning machines are
More efficacious.
The new song's sung
By your billboard controlled
Sisters who nocturnally wreck
Our genetic structure.

II

She's no girl for Bootsie,
This blonde who listens to

The new song, she's more
Like an E. Simms Campbell
Harem princess who's stretched out
On a padded cushion which
Conceals the tentwall covered
Taperecorder which no longer
Plays your song.
She's like ones you used to
See in Narragansett crushing
Gin-dipped olives or pastel pink
Legs akimboed on
Room-sized carpets—
Damning the innate urge
That prods her to alight
Ellington's subway and race
Down 125th to be your
Desdemona, while you stand like
Diz or Miles in cocktail glass
Rooms where you command her brother
Where you face them both
In this Hilton or Sheraton ballroom,
And order greens and chitt'lins.

Dewey Square, 1956

Scrawny-necked black girls
In slingshot shoes, grimy
Hotdog and sauerkraut vendors,
Broken windows where I once wore
The green letter "T"—
And something revolutionary for
Unkinking hair (written in Spanish)
Where the Breyer's ice cream sign
Had been.
All these data lead to the
Conclusion that I
Cannot re-live Brick Bradford
Flash Gordon Jack Armstrong days
When somebody from Kansas
Thought he'd cause Eleanor's
Husband to read want ads

Was it here that I erased
Santa's name with elevator rides
When Macy's truck beat
Daddy home from rehearsal?

It was my Ulysses year
When I sailed the Western
Union A. T. & T. sea from
Columbus Plaza to Herald Square
When I mixed tuna and milk
And chocolate-peanut bars.

But I didn't speak to strangers,
Being a snob in knee pants,
Since none of our family was
On relief or worked for WPA.

But passing the electric eye
Enroute to 7th Avenue (Daddy

Was mad with Ellington) I
Decided to be an electric
Train engineer, but Daddy
Said it was easier
To become a member of
The House of Representatives.

Now, 80 seasons since I
Coveted the cab of the gold
Trimmed black engine, I
Realize that nothing
Has changed but my postal zone.

BLAUPUNKT
(choruses Pepper Adams never took)

Paradiddle, paradiddle flam-
Wham
A toot for Zoot
Six choruses for sweet Rose Cobb
Kadoom kadoom
Ahh Bahh Ahhhh Bahhh Ahhhh Dahh Boo
Bahht Doo Toooo
Make your eyes go white on a
Saturday nite   like Leo Parker
at Club Bali for Paul Mann
'fore Korea —
Pound, Pound — unhuh-huh
Let Gerry Mulligan
make money
while you & Zoot
Make music.
A bahtt for Zoot
tsit, tsit cymballlll
Boo dahh zummm

STEPHEN JONAS

For LeRoi Jones

maybe that "quest thing"
could be "tightened" maybe
my things "have changed too"
maybe   a lot of things
Like now you take out back here:
2 girls bounce ball
against a brickwall avoiding
the scrawl'd to the right of
               white perpendicular
                    "F
                      O
                      U
                      L"-line.

BOOK V

                    As to
"how do you write a poem"
                    you don't
you come to go to hell
by stormy seas in a boat
losing all companions even
        losing the shirt upon yr. back
& darker still it is with some
just a matter of
                    bad blood.
& those(anthologists) can't
just "Leave the Word Alone", If
information can be tampered with
how can you know. The flow
into coherency
        not to be interrupted by
"deletions" or was it a case of
downright
            dishonesty.

(Departing you promised to write
  kissing me full on the lips. I
                    was overcome. Realizing the deep
                affection and warmth
                            that moved you to it .
It is from that same depth
                within me
                            moved me to this Poem.
Drinking together, we discussed Poetry
                and I read you a poem I had
                recently written. Later the conversation
                    fell to pure nonsense which we both pursued
            with equal abandon. Remembering your visit
        I am cheered as I am saddened

                         remembering your departure. Too
                 quickly taken. May it be so with Love
                 which I liken to the Poem.)

That the rhythmic order of the
                          Hellenes be not
      imposed upon the chaotic
                  materials of our daily lives
but that we build within
                  a comparable state of fluidity
to meet that outer state
                          of fluidity
clarity and simplicity are
        the outstanding two characteristics
--defined upon two planes
                  w/a neutral background
and that in building your whatever
that the purpose be
                          opaque
Architecture(Mr. Maximus)
is primarily an art of space,too
Frank L. Wright
but would not fuse Athens or was it
Corinth with steel. Lineal
& dynamic the line should be
and this to be followed by
Sullivan's Law form
            as it does follow
                          function.
From the complex to distill
      a fundamental. The ideal
is human.
            NOTE: Jefferson replacing Athena
                  slaying a giant
                                like a sonnet.
Light more Light
            cried the dying Goethe
that is the binding medium
unites mortar to bricks
holds things together.

If the Poem is difficult to read
it is because the thought producing
the poem was caboose to
        diesel disjunct.
There is too
        the rhythmic occurrence in language
as in and out of the tree
the lines of the vine entwine
    about the lintel
        cross beam
only to terminate
        about me in
the dismal heads
        the caboose
disjunct or just sidetracked/
in all this the native purity is best described into words
    lineal and dynamic
the flow of the line
    should not be interrupted
        the flow of the line   shd. be
    a flow into coherency .
a mathmatic we seek
it is a mathmatic we seek
to reduce to the simple
        the complicated or
would you prefer death:
then"turn up this crooked way,
for in that grove I lafte him"
and this to be followed by
the elongated forms
the distortions of
I suppose his later art
arose
from a know-how
that things in themselves
    have no meaning until
        the imagination plays w/them
and shapes them into
        communicative patterns
intelligible   the structural facts upon

which rests the Poem
are not damn you
                    descriptive columns
Corinthian and Ionic.
What I ask you can our national capitol
            tell us about ourselves
        behind the cool facade
                        classic and eclectic ?
The broken rabble
                of Ahab's crew
come back from the dead
            come back to tell you all
The dead come back
            walking among us
            asking
                asking
        "what is the question"
O do not go to make 'inquisits'
that music with a lying
                        fell
that should cue you
                you who would go back
back to Whitman.
                    Whitman left us
the pyramids or the Stonehedge
The rhythmic recurrences
                    in language
not to be descriptive
                    not to be
as in the arch
where the piers and barrel
            vault support
the contours of the landscape
Yonder's rock's upthrust
    pointing like a finger
cues the architect
        the Poem is no less
Poets should become architects
    of the imagination

to build within
    a comparable state of
    fluidity to meet
an outer state of
                 fluidity.
from the stone head
    the sensual lip of ambition
no word has come
             --burning
  no word
         only the fleck of light
burning in the pupil eye
where he has drilled for light
gives an impression of
        alert awareness
an awareness of eternal light
--lest we forget the eternal repetition
of the eye in the spread fan of
                  the peacock
or the simplicity defined on 2 planes
         with a neutral background.
so that
      nose in the shit like
a sick dog at
        the vomitorium
--considering
        considering the defects
inherent in all
          art-form:
our own national dome, the Hermes
    missing a hand, San Francisco's
  shaky can and Venus
           busted
I have come to build upon my own
mistakes
      thefts
        lies
half mad in the half light
(straining over the bad reproduction)

to see myself
        among those sooty frescoes
in the transepts (Franciscan Basilica)
O Cimabue O Kakuzo
                    dont look back
from yr. uppity air
the sun has blotted out the convulsion
of the anti-christ
figure gestures of mourning women
  and the terrified jews
to a trumpet blast quaking the tombs open
to a cosmic terror.
Purloind that's a word back for it
from the colosseum
structural facts, these are
      to build no to construct damn you
a Farnese Palace
a further design to lure you into the poem
housing
    Edison Marbles
         passages from old narratives
structural lies covered by concrete
facing   a brown painted over
  White House
DEVICE
      this is a design ;
a plan to ' a snake on the brain;
a pattern; an/and
              arrangement of parts
WHAT I'M TELLING YOU IS
                    --forget it

".. AN EAR INJURED BY HEARING THINGS"
(after a statement of Jack Spicer's)

thoughts march
across the page
orderly
the mind
hems & hawes
de-
      fining the line a
metrical dance
not, I caution you
preconceived
free? only
the mind
violating
the law taking
exceptions to
create(never to
new laws(oh,no a
flexibility
it seeks
(tender vine shoots
from the old year's
vine stock(s)
ten-
      tacles up
the wall
feelers out to
the new ways
design?
an arrangement
of parts

mere-
        ly (particulars
of the Poem
traced(for the mind
sketches
technique?
long since
burrowd under
but the pattern
's obvious as are
markings on birds
form? yes
what else
looming before you
underbrush
cleard that the spaces show
clean thru
to a finishd what
have you.

Orgasm 0

               w/outRomans
           (Niew Yorc & Sun in hydra
               darkness—struggle—light
          . . . and out goes the Fool's Canto-
my B.B.C.
          (might at that be a big bad 'orgasm' .) 'But
        you have'nt got that far yet'. You know.
Joel,   (Oppenheimer)   (Outsider 2)
                     in the building of the
Tower of Babel ,
        it wasnt words.
             They run out of flesh. Fresh-maide
wholly by the Word. . . . .
          Law(es) .
             per Boston Blackie No 2 afta Olson's
No.1 ? "I donno." (as is said of my Miltonian
          John of what chapter what
                       verse
        Revelations,
           sez;"I donno".
But, "Jack" to the Boston clack. And the 'theosophy-s'ladies
      . . . . und so on. tho' the old Brunswick wuz as it wuz
sackd about their heels
             (but mind,you,sensible Boston ones. FOR
we WALK, Mister Dorn, and not to
                "Tache a kabe". A strange lyrical
    strain, brought on(I have no doubt-ov-it)
             by the long wide open spaces (George
Stanley's 'blanks'—to borrow one)
          between what else but latin cribs.
(That shd take the wind out ov
            even Miss Moore's
                 prairie skirts.)

(laugh,
motherless sons-of-bitches, the while
Jack Spicer's cultivated
white flowers wither..uncelebrated . . .
I will land you all in Ghandi's Hell—and an
oath (<u>un</u> heard))

THIS IS FOR REAL <u>AND</u> THE VISION IN PAINTING
[(FITZGERALD)
("Marshall, The Doer, Take Command. An Order.
THIS IS NO POEM
THIS IS, JACK . . . FOUR (THE LAW)
ATTENTION. There are Ladies
"PRESENTE."
AMERICA: spit. swine-sty—
[hammer—
(no chisel) .!works!..   "plays with 'm self' and all to
an gyration of hips (Browning, noted it)
not to forget: "this is not to be published:" hand-pressed and hand-
pushd" all as tho' the 'wafer' were to wipe-ass.
(This, a promise I made to Garcia Lorca. To be full-filled
and all the five o'clocks in the afternoons. My God, how much
can You put up with?)
..all for a Hell in four non-discriminatory
colours. .the raw of it.
But, those who have ears
let 'em
or let 'em go   bury their dead. per J.C.
And there is a serious laxity
in New York . . . (that I'm
sure a few Maximus Maxims
might at that cure).
"We shall see" sd. the perhaps blind-man
<u>as contra-jour</u>
oh le fish market. And the "green-grocer"
seems to be passing. Last one, I think wuz,
Kerry Village (South End, but don't say it there..cause they
don't know the Back Bay halts at the New York New Haven Hartford
Ry)   Ole French Quarter . . . Melrose, Lafayette, Knox
(dead end) and St. Cecilia whereis or wuz the

Church of Our Lady of La Victoire. Where ss
the old French Bakery's gone
        and so's the horse-cart w/the chimes
ole Josiah Robinson (now dead, God rest his soul)
      described me with tone and pitch:
                 "ting-ping-
                      ping"
and his hair left back 'ov his bald spot
            "hermetic's" sd.
  Armand. "Kanuck" sd. Josiah and both in the spirit of I
      suppose   yankee spirited competition   and both
bought up to and against the narrower lanes back 'ov
          Winchester St. Worcester
Manchester   Gloucester   all bringing the Roman invasion of the
         Brits into our New England time.
(Poetry? I heard "Poe-tree". .that's locally, but
                    let it ride)
Returning (you follow?
         to Niew Yorc:"so like baby fer-git-it
and dere aint no hope for me neither"
         like Joe Williams. (I
           like the old music) . . .
and Roi, oh Le Roi
       at that would be <u>parfait</u>
        at the <u>Wu</u> court. Elegant in Court dress
to receive the Royal guests . . .
        bowing at the lower-end, (eh, Roi, ?)
so's not to be "cheeky" as the non-conformists
   who bow at the upper end. Like
        this is the "niew day" etc as
"evry day I get the blues"
       read yr ass-paper
         or <u>viva   voce</u> "shut yah
               yap and
I suspect youre a gentile-homme with
        ever-plus of
           heart-tones
"A Jones"
    at that you have the word for it, Sd. Kung. But
I'll be damned if we'll ever get anymore of

them welsh White Rabbits . Sta quiet
Dunn, Joseph, in the hole "they" dug for you . . .
                                at that my Andreas Divus.
        SO   the real problem,
                                        Ed Dorn IS
& what to do between sides.
                        But NOT'tache ah kabe'. Anglo-Saxon
Common Law
        OR, (did'ya heah 'that'?)
                                Henry James, yes,
                & reasons PROPRIETY. Not white-trash
littering a Ben Shahn con-creepin lot . . .
                        radders and chains to teeth-on
Or as my 'bishop' ,Edwardius
                the Marshall:
                                "but not as Classic as
your (meaning 'my') Mrs. Melville Smith. & a 'thank you'
                to the Bishop. You too shall be immortal.
(Not withstanding'losses'   or mis-nomers mis-placed:
                The Rice & Jonah & the Whale Poems (the latter which
,bless my soul, Charles, (Olson) recaptured to me mine. (Oh, ov corze
        it's fun) . . . N'est pas? That was for gertrude
        Stein, who did for herself . . . also fun. Tho' as to the
re/ Jonah and Rico Poems: Whom would you trust to
                        without malice in yr Archives? Respondex
with much s'il vou plais and little more of
                · but do spare us
                        Apologetics, bu jeezus.,
et le space allowed & the hassle w/ the little maggotzines:
        that's U Ouk me et I O uk U seeing we both
                        as tares. J.C. again.
Or the ultimately : where nothin' ever happens, save
        the thickk 'as laard. For whome we must observe
the image's impact would have to be in the sign of the ram,
                        to that is make home. And save yr
        Greek 'n Latin til
                yr see the white
                        of the old timers. What 'timers'
        seem to me passing. At which point, Chaucer might well as
passed over into prose. For, then the Foot is hung-up and well

it might be. . . . but that is the Doctrine and you would not
appreciate it. (Spicer, how the hell do the Dodgers
                  make out there?)   (or to turn on
with Andy Jackson in the 'kitchen cabinet')   Bringing, thus
the return of the white trash ov the
                              shrug-ov-the-shoulder
            (still w/Henry James)
                  blades (but not
          "wind ivah water", Caucaus Mts or
some under world ov the old world   that the Hellenes
                    passed over)
                  For the Azure
yeah, they taking an old word , they new-found-land/ w/sea
         to say   <u>thalassa</u>
                  and for 2 thousand years plus
J.C., the two mythologies, yr gran pappys (not the dirty   dozens)
   that's kaka ..
               Suspect 'Novelty' ; pass on what's Old.
     as to"what's old"?
               See Orgasm (had 'ta
                         go check merself
                         yeah, VII.
And keep those Roman numbers.
                      And also /and Maximus (cagey,
the old fox & the tiger's eye also a real gazz. . but softly ,sir)
   Tho' as to "Baaston": Privy. (Like
a tenth muse)   —still AWOL)   "OUTSIDERS"   <u>sta ferma</u>
   and we like it that way .
               The Gheulfs. Pazzi and latter-day Maffia.
We "dine"
        Wedonot "eat"(unless of course
                some high church mustification of
   Eucharistic mis-
            behavior   and then retire to
"The Rectory"   and Ed Marshall, "The Bishop"
                        prepares yr doctrinale to
   oh Cantabridgian latinity . . .
                but not necessarily
     final resor. Oh I could go on Farther Feeney or
       Kneezy Miller to the "Freshmen" in "the yard."

All, of corse, to further digression.

                          Oh yes, it's still here(The King's
English
          that is)
                 and "the queen" IS
                           MOST conSURVative . . .
(due to neo-Confucian which what. What else?)
                              Sd."Rites"? Yes.
POETRY? Yess. ---and the best (A.B. Spellman) NOT bazeball &
             POOL? --Heavens to Betsy
                  and ov "the hustler" too.)
I do so hate to
          descend to you "people"? For, whereas,
              there is still
The Madonna of the Future,   Henry James or
       Columbia Record Catalog with for 52 & 3, 7 MOZART
Motets for the unaccompanied   male voice, but try to
         get it,   or a
            four letter word, for that matter,
to end this canto: AMOR, but
     not before p.s. to Master's 'ignorance of coin, credit, and
       circulation'. . . .
               finally all is just
downrite ignorance of all matters circulation:
    (& my cat just broke up--Selah
but to still end this canto
              AMOR

A MUDDLE

"Psychology"
  . . . and I look straight at it;
it has no handles. I try to pick it up
     and it slops over. I can't encompass it. It
     is not a dish for the altar. A novel.
Must be, since no historic record
   to give dignity to a vulgar clamour
                to our attention. Careful,tho'
in passing, you note it. Oh, among the un-
precedented occurrences(Book of Divination
    slopping over into a Bestiary) in an age
itself too preoccupied with wonder of the un-
precedented.

A LITTLE MAGIC

you didn't show.
in june you wrote:

"coming by late
      july".

 i layed out the
       manuscripts

and just the right
     books

as Pound did before
for you in that last poem.

july passed and no word.
august stands
       in shallow pools an-
ticipating september
         thot

there is no "you"
i invented

    to say:
"who will come
      afta me

singing as well as i do"?

lens

skill'd metrics
the true
ars poetica

footworks
    minds perculator

lets not
i.e.
    back to

walt whitman's
(blank)

cleft'd foot 'n
half hid 'n

thicket
    's shaggy
        leg .

IV

this entire
    horror shew
so called "free world"

is a paid
    political announcement
brought to you by

the international con-
        spiracy of pronouns
we dare not utter here

for fear of re-
        prisals

<u>what you can see</u>
above
     this branch of the
u.s. post office
(thats a dirty prose line
  upon which hang all the
  obscene
          underneath)

               is
the officious paraclete
          who would
if he were free to
          write
all our poems
        for us

JUNE JORDAN

All the World Moved

All the world moved next to me strange
I grew on my knees
in hats and taffeta trusting
the holy water to run
like grief from a brownstone
cradling.

Blessing a fear of the anywhere
face too pale to be family
my eyes wore ribbons
for Christ on the subway
as weekly as holiness
in Harlem.

God knew no East no West no South
no Skin nothing I learned like
traditions of sin but later
life began and strangely
I survived His innocence
without my own.

Toward a Personal Semantics

if I do take somebody's word on
it means I don't know and you have to
believe if you just don't know

how do I dare to stand as
still as I am still standing

arrows create me
but I am no wish

after all the plunging
myself is no sanctuary
birds feed and fly inside me shattering
the sullen spell of any
accidental

eyeless storm to twist and sting
the tree of my remaining
like the wind

San Juan

Accidental far into the longer light
or smoking
clouds that lip whole hillsides
spoken nearly foliated full
a free green raveling alive
as blue as pale
as rectilinear

the red the eyebrow
covering a privacy a space
particular ensnarement
flowering roulette

place opening knees night water

color the engine air
on Sunday
silhouette the sound

and silently

some miles away the mountain
the moon
the same

Bus Window

bus window
show himself a
wholesale florist rose somebody
help the wholesale
dollar blossom spill to soil
low pile
on wanton windowsills
whole
saleflorists seedy
decorations startle   small

BOB KAUFMAN

I Have Folded My Sorrows

I have folded my sorrows into the mantle of summer night,
Assigning each brief storm its allotted space in time,
Quietly pursuing catastrophic histories buried in my eyes.
And yes, the world is not some unplayed Cosmic Game,
And the sun is still ninety-three million miles from me,
And in the imaginary forest, the shingled hippo becomes
        the gay unicorn.
No, my traffic is not with addled keepers of yesterday's
        disasters,
Seekers of manifest disembowelment on shafts of yesterday's
        pains.
Blues come dressed like introspective echoes of a journey.
And yes, I have searched the rooms of the moon on cold
        summer nights.
And yes, I have refought those unfinished encounters.
        Still, they remain unfinished.
And yes, I have at times wished myself something different.

The tragedies are sung nightly at the funerals of the poet;
The revisited soul is wrapped in the aura of familiarity.

East Fifth Street (N.Y.)

Twisting brass, key of G, tenement stoned,
Singing Jacob's song, with Caribbe emphasis.

Flinging the curls of infant rabbis, gently,
Into the glowing East Side night.

Esther's hand, in Malinche's clasped,
Traps the fly of evening, forever.

Ancient log-rolling caps of Caribbe waves
Splashing crowded harbors of endless steps.

Angry fire-eyed children clutch transient winds,
Singing Gypsy songs, love me now, love me now.

The echoes return, riding the voice of the river,
AS TIME CRIES OUT, ON THE SKIN OF AN African drum.

Lorca

Split ears of morning earth green now,
Love and death twisted in tree arms,
    Come love, throw out your nipple
to the teeth of a passing clown.

Spit olive pits at my Lorca.
Give Harlem's king one spoon,
At four in the never noon.
Scoop out the croaker eyes
    of rose flavored Gypsies
Singing García,
In lost Spain's
Darkened noon.

Picasso's Balcony

Pale morning light, dying in shadows, loving the earth in midday rays,
casting blue to skies in rings, sowing powder trails across balconies.
Hung in evening to swing gently, on shoulders of time, growing old, yet
swallowing events of a thousand nights of dying and loving, all blue.
Gone to that tomb, hidden in cubic air, breathing sounds of sorrow.

Crying love rising from the lips of wounded flowers, wailing, sobbing,
breathing uneven sounds of sorrow, lying in wells of earth, throbbing,
covered with desperate laughter, out of cool angels, spread over night.
Dancing blue images, shades of blue pasts, all yesterdays, tomorrows,
breaking on pebbled bodies, on sands of blue and coral, spent.

Life lying heaped in mounds, with volcano mouth tops, puckered, open,
sucking in atoms of air, sprinkling in atoms of air, coloring space, with
flecks of brilliance, opaline glistening, in eyes, in flames.

Blue flames burning, on rusty cliffs, overlooking blue seas, bluish. In sad
times, hurt seabirds come to wail in ice white wind, alone, and wail in
starlight wells, cold pits of evening, and endings, flinging rounds of flame
sheeted balls of jagged bone, eaten, with remains of torn flowers, over-
whelming after-thoughts, binding loves, classic pains, casting elongated
shadows, of earthly blue.

Stringing hours together in thin melodic lines, wrapped around the pearl
neck of morning, beneath the laughter, of sad sea birds.

NOVELS FROM A FRAGMENT IN PROGRESS

RETURN TRIP SEATED ERECT ON THE SINGING TRAIN IN
    [DELIBERATE
ATTEMPT NOT TO FALL ASLEEP, USE OF IMAGINATION TO
    [AVOID SWAYING
PEOPLE, UNREAL VISIONS OF MURALS ON RED RESTROOM
    [FLOORS, SLEEP
URGE GETTING STRONGER, SCREWING UP THE EYES TO
    [A PERFECT BREAST,
ROUGH STOP, STRONG WISH FOR EROTICISM DEPARTING
    [NATIONS CARRYING
BIG PAPER BAGS, WONDERING ABOUT THE DENTS IN
    [BOXER'S FACES,
REJECTION OF THE SEXUAL ASPECT OF SWEAT, PICTURE
    [OF THE MOTORMAN
AS THE MYSTIC FERRYMAN, HIS FACE WOULD EVER BE
    [DESCRIBED IN
NOVELS, AWARENESS OF MUSIC OUT BY THE WHEELS,
    [SERIOUS ATTEMPT TO
WRITE SONGS, SURPRISED AT MY OWN NAIVETE, AMUSED
    [BY SOUNDS LIKE
ONE I CAN'T WRITE, APPROACHING STATION, EYES OF
    [SLIDING DOOR,
WAITING FOR IT TO OPEN, MORE PEOPLE, ANOTHER STOP.
    [IT ALWAYS
HAPPENS, BRING THIS OFF WITHOUT ANNOYING. ALWAYS
    [WATCH THEM GET
OFF BEFORE THE BIG EVENT, I ALMOST GIVE UP AT TIMES
    [LIKE THESE.
HOW TO SAVE IT. REPETITIOUS FRUSTRATION, NOW,
    [MYTHIC HOURS

WITHOUT LOSING A GRIP ON MY SANITY & FREQUENTLY,
  [WOMEN REALIZE MY
CONCENTRATION TO MASTER THIS TRICK, WILLING TO
  [RIDE PAST THEIR
DESTINATION.

THE CELEBRATED WHITE-CAP SPELLING BEE

THE CELEBRATED WHITE-CAP SPELLING BEE WAS WON
    [BY A SPELLING BEE.
A STAR ASKED A POINTED QUESTION: CAN A CIRCLE WRAP
    [AROUND ITSELF?
A STILLED PYGMY ANSWERS, FROM THE BACK OF MY
    [MIND, ARE WE DEEP DWARFS
AND HAVE OUR SAY IN THE AFFAIRS OF FLOWERS, A
    [MISSPELLLED BEE MAKES A SIGN.
BLUE IS ONE OF THE MANY FACES OF BLUE. HOW QUICK A
    [RED WHALE SINGS THE BLUES.
WHEN AN OUTBOARD SOLAR BOAT SINKS, I WILL WALK
    [THE SUN'S PERIMETER, CURVING UP.
ONCE I PUT MY INITIALS ON A MAGNIFICENT CROCODILE.
WE WALKED A RIVER'S FLOOR. A BIRD I HEARD SING IN A
    [TREE IN THE GULF OF MEXICO . . .
BIRD SONG OF LOVELY SALT, A LOVE SONG.
I CHANGE MY MIND, AND THE NEW ONE IS OLDER . . . A
    [DRUM BEATS
BEHIND MY RIBS.

SOMEONE DREW A PORTRAIT ON A WAVE . . . IT WOVE AS
    [WE PASSED, DOING KNOTS, RUST HANDS.
SWELLS STOP WHEN THE SEA IS ALARMED. HELL COOLS
    [ITS FIRES OF ANTICIPATION.
WHEN OCEANS MEET, OCEANS BELOW, REUNIONS OF
    [SHIPS, SAILORS, GULLS, BLACK-HAIRED GIRLS.
THE SEA BATHES IN RAIN WATER, MORNING, MOON &
    [LIGHT, THE CLEAN SEA.
GREAT FARMS ON THE OCEAN FLOOR, GREEN CROPS OF
    [SUNKEN HULLS GROWING SHELLS.
SEAS THAT GROW FROM A HOLE BORN IN A TURTLE'S
    [BACK, A SEA IN A TORTOISE SACK.

FISH GO NAKED ALL THEIR LIVES. WHEN CAUGHT, THEY
    [DIE OF EMBARRASSMENT.
MANY, MANY YEARS AGO, THERE WERE MANY, MANY
    [YEARS TO GO & MANY, MANY MILES TO COME.
THE LAND IS A GREAT, SAD FACE. THE SEA IS A HUGE
    [TEAR, COMPASSION'S TWINS.

IF THERE IS A GOD BENEATH THE SEA, HE IS DRUNK AND
    [TELLING FANTASTIC LIES.
WHEN THE MOON IS DRINKING, THE SEA STAGGERS LIKE
    [A DRUNKEN SAILOR.
POETS WHO DROWN AT SEA, THEMSELVES, BECOME
    [BEAUTIFUL WET SONGS, CRANE.
A LOOKOUT MAKES A LANDFALL, A FALLING LAND MAKES
    [A LOOKOUT.
AT THE ENDS OF THE WATER, THE HOLY MARRIAGE OF
    [THE HORIZONS.
THE SEA, DILUTED CONTINENTS LOVING FALLEN SKIES,
    [TIME BEFORE
TIME, TIME PAST, TIME COMING INTO TIME. TIME
    [NOW, TIME TO
COME, TIMELESS, FLOWING INTO TIME.
EVERYTHING IS THE SEA. THE SEA IS EVERYTHING,
    [ALWAYS . . .
ETERNALLY, I SWEAR.

Oregon

You are with me Oregon,
Day and night, I feel you, Oregon.
I am Negro. I am Oregon.
Oregon is me, the planet
Oregon, the state Oregon, Oregon.
In the night, you come with bicycle wheels,
Oregon you come
With stars of fire. You come green.
Green eyes, hair, arms,
Head, face, legs, feet, toes
Green, nose green, your
Breasts green, your cross
Green, your blood green.
Oregon winds blow around
Oregon. I am green, Oregon.
Oregon lives in me,
Oregon, you come and make
Me into a bird and fly me
To secret places day and night.
The secret places in Oregon,
I am standing on the steps
Of the holy church of Crispus
Attucks St. John the Baptist,
the holy brother of Christ,
I am talking to Lorca. We
Decide the Hart Crane trip, home to Oregon
Heaven flight from Gulf of
Mexico, the bridge is
Crossed, and the florid black found.

A Terror Is More Certain

A terror is more certain than all the rare desirable popular songs i know,
than even now when all of my myths have become . . . , & walk around in
black shiny galoshes & carry dirty laundry to & fro, & read great books
& don't know criminals intimately, & publish fat books of the month &
have wifeys that are lousy in bed & never realize how bad my writing is
because i am poor & symbolize myself.

A certain desirable is more terror to me than all that's rare, How come
they don't give an academic award to all the movie stars that die? They're
still acting, ain't they? Even if they are dead, it should not be held against
them, after all they still have the public on their side, how would you like
to be a dead movie star & have people sitting on your grave?

A rare me is more certain than desirable, that's all the terror, there are
too many basketball players in this world & too much progress in the bur-
ial industry, let's have old fashioned funerals & stand around and forgive
& borrow wet handkerchiefs and sneak out for drinks & help load the guy
into the wagon, & feel sad & make a date with the widow & believe we
don't see all of the people sinking into the subways going to basketball
games & designing baby sitters at Madison Square Garden.

A certain me is desirable, what is so rare as air in a Poem, why can't i
write a foreign movie like all the other boys my age, I confess to all the
crimes committed during the month of April, but not to save my own
neck, which is adjustable, & telescopes into any size noose, I'm doing it to
save Gertrude Stein's reputation, who is secretly flying model airplanes
for the underground railroad stern gang of oz, & is the favorite in all the
bouts . . . not officially opened yet Holland tunnel is the one who writes
untrue phone numbers.

A desirable poem is more than rare, & terror is certain, who wants to be a
poet & work a twenty four hour shift, they never ask you first, who wants
to listen to the radiator play string quartets all night. I want to be allowed

not to be, suppose a man wants to swing on kiddie swings, should people be allowed to stab him with queer looks & drag him off to bed & its no fun on top of a lady when her hair is full of shiny little machines & your ass reflected in that television screen, who wants to be a poet if you fuck on t.v. & all those cowboys watching.

UNHISTORICAL EVENTS

APOLLINAIRE
    NEVER KNEW ABOUT ROCK GUT CHARLIE
    WHO GAVE FIFTY CENTS TO A POLICEMAN
    DRIVING AROUND IN A 1927 NASH

APOLLINAIRE
    NEVER MET CINDER BOTTOM BLUE,
    FAT SAXOPHONE PLAYER WHO LAUGHED
    WHILE PLAYING AND HAD STEEL TEETH

APOLLINAIRE
    NEVER HIKED IN PAPIER MACHE WOODS
    AND HAD A SCOUTMASTER WHO WROTE A SONG
        [ABOUT
    IVORY SOAP AND HAD A BAPTIST FUNERAL

APOLLINAIRE
    NEVER SAILED WITH RIFF RAFF ROLFE
    WHO WAS RICH IN CALIFORNIA, BUT
    HAD TO FLEE BECAUSE HE WAS QUEER

APOLLINAIRE
    NEVER DRANK WITH LADY CHOPPY WINE,
    PEERLESS FEMALE DRUNK, WHO TALKED TO SHRUBS
    AND MADE CHILDREN SING IN THE STREETS

APOLLINAIRE
    NEVER SLEPT ALL NIGHT IN AN ICEHOUSE,
    WAITING FOR SEBASTIAN TO RISE FROM THE
        [AMMONIA
    TANKS
    AND SHOW HIM THE LITTLE UNPAINTED ARROWS.

The Biggest Fisherman

singular prints filed along damp banks,
supposed evidence of fouled strings, all,

breached dikes of teeth hewn agate statues
scaly echoes in eroded huts of slate and gristle.

Mildewed toes of pastoral escapes, mossy charades,
cane towered blind, smooth blister on watern neck

angry glowing fish in eniwetok garments and pig tusks
alarmed horror of black croakers, finned hawks sinking.

collectors of fresh teeth and souls of night vision demons
taxidermy fiesta of revolutionary aquatic holidays lost.

breeding hills of happy men, of no particular bent, or none,
condemned to undreamlike beauty of day to day to day,
deprived of night, ribbon waves of newly glowing fish.

CROOTY SONGO

DERRAT SLEGELATIONS, FLO GOOF BABER,
SCRASH SHO DUBIES, WAGO WAILO WAILO.
GEED BOP NAVA GLIED, NAVA GLIED NAVA,
SPLEERIEDER, HUYEDIST, HEDACAZ, AX—,O,O.

DEEREDITION, BOOMEDITION, SQUOM, SQUOM, SQUOM.
DEE BEETSTRAWIST, WAPAGO, LOCOEST, LOCORO, LO.
VOOMETEYEREEPETIOP, BOP, BOP, BOP, WHIPOLAT.

DEGET, SKLOKO, KURRITIF, PLOG, MANGI, PLOG MANGI,
CLOPO JAGO BREE, BREE, ASLOOPERED, AKINGO LABY.
ENGPOP, ENGPOP, BOP, PLOLO, PLOLO, BOP, BOP.

THE LATE LAMENTED WIND, BURNED IN INDIGNATION

TONTO IS DEAD, TONTO IS DEAD, TONTO IS DEAD
    RUN HIDE IN SUBWAYS.
    ELECTRIC ARROW OF PENITENT MACHINES & FOOT-
STEP
    HORROR
  LET THE FLEA CIRCUS PERFORM, TONTO IS DEAD-

THE BEST PLACE TO JUDGE A TAP DANCE CONTEST,
    IS FROM BENEATH THE STAGE.
    TONTO IS DEAD, HIDE IN SUBWAYS.
HEAVY WATER MUSIC, SPILLED FROM PUBLIC
    [HARPSICHORDS,

AT GALA LAUNDERMAT CONCERTS, FEATURING SONATAS
    [FOR
DE-
    FEATED OBOES,
    BETWEEN DOOR SLAM OVERTURES, & SOGGY BALLETS,
    EXITING INTO KEY EYES OF LONELY JAZZERS,
      TONTO IS DEAD, TONTO IS DEAD,
        MUSEUMS ARE EXEMPT FROM MARTIAL LAW,
        HIDE IN THE SUBWAY, QUICK
          BEFORE IT MELTS.

ELOUISE LOFTIN

A Black Lady

She sat on the Lex line #2
pink patent crossed feet
and goodluck fish danglin
from the wrist
Say hello
calmly nod but no more
cause she don't play with kids
Pink patent crossed feet
crust on one knee ash layin
in the thumb
How far down is she goin
Where is she comin from
and how far down is backin up
Stop starin
would if you could
but can't
cause spirits in her eyes say
she goin to the stop where you can
say more
and she don't have to hold
that bag so tight

What Sunni Say

shoot me for
the moon through
the burning spreading head
open me up the me of me
put it inside where i need
let me carry it around
all day
taste like it the night
all long and songless
smell like it into
the nights of
next week's need

bkln

at a house no. 99
and a sign on the window
NDIAN JO RLGIE
      ARTICLES
and a letterdrop
and a note on the door
"dear jo
aint seen you since rabbit
coats come in style
all these mornins i leaned
against your padlock and peepin
through the blinds seems like more
than me is tryin to get next to you.

man, if you in there dead you
better say somethin"

Barefoot Necklace

empty the pain
and what i believe of you
unsaid in words. An investment
to the world in the world
unfound. unsafe. only the pedestrian act
assuming air breathing
and dying. what temporary grace
my reality allows me. and you
inside your body   mad scars
and dancing a pitted tamborine
that will not play for the absence
of words my words though i sing
a tangled pantomine of dreams
under the sparrows knees.
alone you are yourself
a history and desire of what
in the world you will show as yourself
myself alone is who i am
a barefoot necklace
who cannot come in
alone unless twisted
by who i believe i am
or even myself to be
a space where in your neck
empty. the spirit gone
i would come
if only to raise the sparrow

april '68

the ball bearings fell out
of my roller skates,
I sat close to the tv
my 7 month baby in my arms
the veil I wore to her father's
funeral in her mouth and hands
behind me my mother blue roses
on a faded house dress growing
up in her lap watered with her
tears running from her eyes
like beads on a necklace falling
in a bowl of collards
amerikkk amerikkka reach out
and touch your tv sets high
school graduation is just around
the conor

scabible
after a nixon–baily duet

rows of piggy bank fed coins
headless yo-yo's in an apple pie
fingers desecrates piano
calves cool out with a spoon
hit-man issued to barb-wire moon

hey diddle diddle
watch your fiddle

N. J. LOFTIS

from *Black Anima*

Changes — One

And I sit here
    for five days now
sit here in prison
for running a stoplight in election year
the soiled sunlight from the street
    hard against the vision
piss pouring into latrine
like blood into a butcher's pail

And went on hunger strike
to protest conditions
    how draft dodgers denied
entry to minimum security
were used as prostitutes
how a man was hung
    with hands tied behind his back
and they called it suicide

And I recognized them
    in the prison library
recognized Malcolm and King
reading from a strange history
the book of our collective dream

"Look," said King
here is Gonga-Mussa
on his pilgrimage to Mecca
this town, his retainers
    60,000 in all
these are the eight camels carrying gold
"And here," said Malcolm

is Cinquez among the founding fathers
    and this figure here
bound in mummy cloth
is your grandfather who is dead
We who are no longer
    yet seem to be
here have the one vision
though in life we were known
    only for our opposition,
the poet among his people
the active man among his books
the single city reached by
    a thousand winding entries

Take this ring
all of whose parts have a common center
joining what's to come
with what has been
    and give it to your bride
whom you shall meet in Africa

And:

Changes — Five

No, no Shakespeare not your gloomy melancholy. *To be or not to be* is a
kink you've cleverly cast in the body's machine which takes everything in
and shits it all out again, a sideshow like midget-wrestling or fat ladies
rubbing bellies to distract us from the real tragedy. That shadowy being
we see ranting before us on the stage is too much like us to be taken as
mere "play," and, perhaps,

too much like you, busy contemplating the visible reality, while a mind-
less destiny that a star-haunted heaven has written in indecipherable cal-
ligraphy, a heaven lamenting with convulsive stars, has gently attached it-
self to you from without.

It is all too proximate to be funny, or merely amusing. Today a musical
would be made to wean us from its piercing sting, the dread terror of the
thing, truth too real to be ignored, too protracted to be acted upon. For-
tunately, the dead only return to us in grade "B" movies, dreams, or po-
ets' imaginings, permitting us the luxury of postponing true perception
of reality indefinitely, until another life, if need be, or to twist it into a
shape that agrees with our fantasies. Still, suppose a bright billboard ap-
peared in the sky reading: THIS IS YOUR IDENTITY. Oh, how I
would delight to see the homosexual and the he-man delighting in what a
homosexual and a he-man should be. Lacking this clear certainty, the
surety of birds of passage cracking open hostile skies as a crack goes
through a cup, we abandon our true being, being existing solely for itself,
not needing the other to confine or define it from without, being all es-
sence without a rim.

It is time to take inventory. You've packed the luggage and left the key
next door. Plane at eleven. Auden's for tea. What time is it? Three. Time
to take inventory. The library at six. Leaving there by taxi. It is time,

time to examine the very ground on which we walk, to examine the room
settling about your shoulders at afternoon, to examine it through and

through: to see. But even this is illusory if you cannot annihilate the sub-
tle dependencies that anticipate the object seen, surmising all its fate, its
character and mental state without once staring it face to face, or noticing
its body's distinct from the mask it placed on its head to deceive you.

Until that frontier where you can see the dizzy depths from which earth
is always uprooting itself, where momentary and cosmic meet, connecting
the simple and transitory "me" with eternity, you must awake nightly
with the shriveled head of a limp dream, you must content yourself not
simply with being, but swapping shapes with the things surrounding you,
for how else shall you know them, since the ground is corroded where
you might have detached yourself from the muddle of images attacking
you and surveyed the whole, the "To-Ti," from its vague beginning in
history right down to its present uncertainty.

You must complete the death begun in you, plunging to hell, if that's
what you must do, before you can release yourself from that protean em-
pathy with your locality, before you stand anew at the end of dreams on
the very Ground of Being from which the roses spring, not just a point
on the ring but the ring itself.

But all that is far from where you are right now, walking down Broadway
toward the subway, the scrawny tree becomes you, not decking itself out
like queen, but exchanging its being with yours until the piss pours on
you that erodes the bark away, and the cool winds seem to tear off your
limbs.

You are the tree that is pissed upon and the dog that pisses, demanding
red meat three times a day, your right to lie where and with whom you
wish, shelter when sunlight makes a pyre of the leaves, a human hand to
scratch your belly when it brings delight. Yes, you know your rights. The
moon and other heavenly bodies no longer concern you, who bay only
when human kindness turns to aggression, only at the demeaning invec-
tives against your breed, indeed, against everything dog denotes: "dog-
gone," "dog take ya," "dog damn." What you're asking is a reversal of
things, to be treated not as men, but as gods, so that the last more fully
may be first, for even your name is god in reverse.

You wiggle free from that shape but as you descend the subway stair, a
butterfly flutters up here and there, you too flounce sillily from thought

to thought, flirting with new meaning before the old has properly ex-
hausted its being. Your arms expand to wing. Your hazel eyes are speckled
with spots of light.

You have become what you dreamed.

Changes — Eight

And one day Hughes said
    "I've known rivers ancient as the world and older
than the
        flow of human blood in the veins"

thus cutting across time's withershins
the combustible leaves of *Crises*
    like the processional reds and golds
    of autumn ablaze in the crypt forest

Atropos cutting the thread
    weaving the light against it
and Rosy living in London said
to her reclining Sappho
"I told Langston he'd be dead at sixty
if he didn't stop eating"

        the swollen corpse adrift
          on the black tide
       time's knot tied and untied
          as it rose and fell
          the half-submerged belly
          blown out like a sail

Time sifts the wheat from the chaff
    and the rat from the wheat:
    and Tolson first traced the course
where the rainbow arched to its source
plunging to the pitch and pith of things
containing more of alchemy than a witch's sabbath

The shadow swimming vaguely
in the Library's light
    gathering the gold against them
a few friends and you break bread

attended by all the resident dead
    that line the bookstalls
    that's what poetry is (Auden)

or maybe it was Lenny Horn,
a bridge between the dead and the unborn
"So you are going to Egypt
    to resurrect Ikhnaton's tomb"
The words pass through you
falling on a stony place where nothing blooms
Outside, the saffron sunlight swims
    toward you in concentric circles
    as day goes down

Then Chesnutt, let his ladder down,
    down into the leper commune
his mind shattered by the gale
of images, picking and choosing identities
as at a rummage sale

You memorized your lesson well
pointing it out in detail
    to others in your company
trying to tell them how Mphahlele
and Spender unwittingly (perhaps)
were cuddled by the CIA

Imagine climbing all your childhood
toward some promontory
    where you dreamed the white cliffs
    shot up out of the bickering spray
only to find when arriving there
what you dreamed had gone away
    or perhaps never existed
and what remains is only a cheap
and mean province open to all comers

You would make of that paltry place
the thing you always dreamed
who else but Mphahlele could praise
    Joseph C. so openly

thereby renouncing his birthright
on the banks of the Nile
and swap the sculptured beauty of Nefertiti
swap it for the bulges of Queen Vicky

Imamu (LeRoi) saw it all six
    years ago at the Black Arts
        before fools fell upon the place
           "Your gonna have to forget
    everything taught you down in Tennessee"
Malcolm was just dead and maggots
spreading their whiteness over his cold body

What whiteness shall we add
to this whiteness like sterile clouds
    bellowing dryly over the Pentagon?
    I'll tell you
the whiteness of fear
flashing across the hunter's face
when he is no longer hunter but quarry

Were it not for for the glory
said Marlowe. Were it not for the glory . . .
    Makers of history they.
    We, those to whom it happens.
Straw men bending
when the gale blowing gently
shakes the wheat from the chaff

On the banks of the Seine
    the spell shall be broken
Prospero's wand shattered in two
    and tossed out to sea.
Yes a tempest is afoot
    that he won't survive so easily

        Caliban! Caliban!
        Blow your horn, man

              TAXI TAXI TAXI

CLARENCE MAJOR

Paragraph from English Speaking World

it is the wish of the general
public
to conclude that
you enjoy
your inferiority
chance to be seen
-your televised drunks
your fifteen cents whitman
comic book
jazz (monk, powell, etc)
in small mechanizations

tho at the beginning
i could have told millions
anxious to juggle human crap
into the earth
of society (the rich earth receiveth all)
that
you did not, technologically, take
no shit

off nobody

A Petition for Langston Hughes

his alliance was fragmented.
Ishmael Reed & I stood at the foot
of his steps, established. Drunk:
He sent me a check just before the tactics ended
        I checked: black caucus community *simple*
takes a century to stop laughing.
Planners of the give away, between white grants
& partnerships. "I'm not qualified to remember
excuses, activists may have turned away.
I am beyond, part left scoffing. Balanced
and uneducated, unbalanced, Hughes was not my hero
tho I sensed he was a Representation. Could
have majored, demands of circumvented black arts
for self-determination of the future of black art
as black art/black art. The process of the big sea
& harlem of no human neighbors
(I wonder if anybody in that block of brownstones
structured with eyes his grandness, downtown?)
The anthologies I got pissed off about, that were
never published. The planning was for tax escapes;
Africa was a valley, the white man one to take
in focus with ease, without revolution. Crying black
blood, persistent thrusts of a lukewarm proposal.
Singing & wondering as one wonders.
        Somebody else to take up from
Ah fuck it!

Media on War
or, the square root of vietnam

did these flyers
of everybody's flag
every nation's real-
estate   finish eating into
the rear of our birth-
right. where did they come from.

they come with this their line
that damsnap our end and no

soundtrack shall stand
emotionless or otherwise
able to believe (our

ears

Edge Guide for Impression

I
groped
around   in the dust
black stale airless basement
of time
and accident
in search
of the
pipes: of logic
which
connect somehow the failure
of yester
day
to the failure
of today
and accidentally
found darkness
and love

News Story

Heard over the radio:
    a white woman from Can./with
    sticks of dina
    mite trans ported from Can.
    (Her home
    &
some serious Afro-Americans
(called NEGROES
                   were uncovered
    but not in bed.
by the curious group
titled FBI
        In a plot to BLOW   UP
               BLOWUP
               BOM
               BLAM
items listed:
Lady Lib
Lib Bell
Wash Monu. Etc
           Teach "our" country a thing or 2 ???
If the serious saboteurs
had succeeded/ who could say
    We would not have a deeper sense of reality
& self

A Poem Americans Are Going to Have to Memorize Soon

these huge teachable slangy people
touched with giddy shallowness (dig

the substance of American Humor, defraud
even plants in their own humble sunlight
like in apartment windows, even parcels
for real people who go deep,
in irregular bareness even into some gods or the mind
become

monstrosities, you know
money, chairs and things like the meaning of other
people are not even accessible DESTRUCTION here)

threadbare in this revolution
now submissively jump into some cold practice,

brash enough to have appointments
official like, while I lay up digging this shit

Education by Degrees

The wedge inside your ease
begins to come cancerous: and you do
not wonder longer or now,
why, the face of discontent is broken:
twisted, broken, why the placenta cord shrinks;
the cartridges of your hatred; you do not
wonder at the hemorrhaging of your own brain;
you and I and all of us know
there is inside the oilproofed antibodies
a pointless accumulation of lubrication.
Yet distilled we are not moved, we wait
for nutrition or infection—it does not matter.
The spirit of our sperm is so basic we
      have not given it a thought.
We remain captive. Not even by our own rot
are we skinned to the point of care.
I face a mirror transferred inside
my own breathing and watch the hair grow
on my own unwillingness to lie to you.

Not This—This Here!

print documentcheap ink said
horoscope to flesheyes I
am "that I—not this I
      he AM) that is
would like to live
would   like living in, rather thru
the Spring, Summer of some
new england

                maple sugar shoe
                make shops water-
                front lobstermen
                rich children elec-
                tronics workers nantucket
                TIME

there is no sign
A SIGN that shows somewhere
in sand, aside

how far rome is
is moscow is calcutta is bombay
no sign registering what

it is like. His "me horo
scope talks about that ARTLESS VAGUE
scar on paper,   not this

Mortal Roundness

this: the nagging way
a weak bulb 60 watt pesters the
sophisticated skin edge rough hair on the skin edge
on the circlebone, protects the hair over his
disobedient light eye. It,
a unit of electric cool-
ness, equal to the ampere
:equal to the volt
! Equal to the pressure.   Is a rim, mortal
roundness, part-
icular. Diminish-
ing in jumps-

mottled, when it *talks* to imprint
him. (Or you
        You see we are sitting here in this room

        YET YOU CANNOT SEE US WE
        See you

.Under such stern word sculling of his particular
verbal
anthro-
PO
LOGICAL   (& simple "rational" way he goes
       beyond
your glibdumb manipulations,   ("you people
they say
       (Are like funnystores.

JUSTICE TRANSLATES ENGLISH INTO EACH NERVOUS
   [VERB of

      "I remember merit" .   earned. So much for
        so little value, intrinsic we need

not go that far in:
to it: like
th
is

SO THIS NOTHING ELSE TURNS A COMPLETE NAME
[WHEEL THAT

ENDS NOWHERE outside the body the last

STRAW & the
<u>first</u>

Pictures

Negro girls
like 12 years old, in
    [enclaves]
midwest ENDS
    in integrated
LIQUID SLANG BRANCHES OF TERMINAL BRICKS
that is, integrated in-
to   the red bricks of these
    years,
behind TV voices animating clumsy
    THE CLUE TO MY JUDGment
report of BLACK respiration
    confuse their soft
solid simplicity, & they carry white
    wallets, they do not
carry pictures of **light** in these
    their INTEGRATED heaviness

coming clearly back to a simple/sound
    MOTIVE for
carrying snapshots of friends
    fallout beautiful if they now
see the lineage loveliness of THEMSELVES
    & schoolmates as any face

Water USA

america, tom sawyer, is bigger
than your swim
hole. You meant, the union, water-
falls. one waterfall
a path near, from which you
jump, folklore, holding
your nose. a chemical change
takes place as you pollute
the water i drink. as your
jet lands, crashing my
environment. tom sawyer can't hold
all the dead bodies upright
nor get anything
out of a lecture on control
systems. and bigger
thomas didn't have an even
chance to study chemistry

LEROY MCLUCAS

Negotiation

imagine   dinin   car
union railways
boot servin
brandy
in
walk
booker t
"Wha u wan? ed'kashun"

Graph

Armfull bedwork carbonized
delinquent ejaculation
fornicated ghetto
hardbound idiom
jackass jacknife jackoff jackscrew
jailbird jaywalker jazzer jeer jesse
jame jivejitterbug jobseeker john
joiner joggler juggler junkman
knottyknight leaseless lofer
muddymule nughtnymphs
outrooted pantaloon
quarter rubber stamp
tenderfootin umbrella
vaginal woebegone
x yesman zulu

OLIVER PITCHER

Why don't we rock the casket here in the moonlight?

A man begins in the cradle and ends in the casket. That's if he's a two time winner. In between? The echo of a long lament. A mosaic of sleep. A marble laugh. A few grapes. A short wail from the other shore. The scattered moldy crumbs of best intentions and the insecure peace of distance. The moon and the sun go on playing an eternal game. Show-me-yours and I'll-show-you-mine but words fail us. We say, here lies a man in a telephone booth, already cold and without direct communication to the moon to warm himself. And rock so soon!

Rock, rock, rock the casket here in the moonlight.

Dust of Silence

This is the hour the pale and neutral moon
    pricked by the Stygian traffics flobs
    to the gutted out yards, front and
    back. This is the hour young men with
    store houses congested with empty pic-
    ture frames for heads, walk the dusty
    roads in stocking feet. Their canvasses
    are tattered to cards of identity
    scattered upon the sea . . .

Smithereens of sound is now dust of silence . . . slowly fallen upon the
roofs and this street like a parental hush; heavily, the imperial mantle . . .
At ten A. M. after the dishes were washed and Christ had been hanging
makeshiftly from a cross for hours, (silenced as effectively as our neigh-
bor's dearly-beloved rope, even though we knew it would happen and did
happen) it was this way. Heliotrope scented silence sneaked between these
cell houses near Calvary, into those sties and these chicken coops.
Goldleaf chickens cocked their heads and perched on one leg longer than
they normally would. Distant spurts of light, puffs of lightning or vague
suggestions of incendiaries? only the penumbras could be seen far off on
the thin black strip of horizon of Calvary Hill. But only a few saw, and
from the corner of their eyes. It was darkly this way on this and certain
other streets at ten A. M. when an oxblood dawn kept its grip on the city,
the morning German boys having their boyish prank were expected to
march through the Arc de Triomphe, even though we knew it would hap-
pen, and did happen. This hush pervades now, heavily, the reciprocal
hush; the dripping faucet silences: the dust, the sovereign dust. Car noises
are heard, yes, a faint rumble of trucks, buses languid in their freedom,
but they remain distant, engines balking at their reins, sniffing, not at all
sure they want to come through this narrow, one-way street, they would
be trespassing on roofs, engine, arc, chickens, all stamped GUILTY BY
ASSOCIATION, a clay pox from dust un-risen on drizzling Easter . . .
Who slammed that door?! What defiance! . . The sound sends out a warn-
ing tremor of an impending bolt of violence; on a window sill where gera-
niums and dust mops are flowering, a geranium shivers. The cooper

across the street, standing in the arch entrance to his shop, made a few
half-hearted taps on a barrel he was making earlier this morning, but now
he has disappeared in the blackness of his shop where he keeps the light
off. For years the sound of the fireworks has been heard in the distance,
and it will remain this way, everyone is sure of it, so there is no cause for
alarm since no one knows what day is being celebrated, and there is safety
in silence.

Now is the moment a gray hand streaks across
        this slate of sky; catch the beggar's
        ransom of dreams!

                the aged have outbursts now

the moment of dog eared statistics hesitating a
        moment before their consecration into dust

                        now the aged squawk, feather
                        flayed birds; the screeech
                        and screeech and screech
                        to out-sound the clack of
                        their joints and bones in
                        their ricky ticky music

now the Kewpie Doll ascends the throne; the
        scene is shifted!

                        the aged complain of the vibra-
                        tions coming from the caves beneath
                        cellars; and everyone hears! now

The Generation two-timely plucked, thereby born
        OUT OF GENERATION quickly tape the aged and
        soundproof like mummies until they promise
        a better display of manners they taught
        and now all muster a twenty-one fart salute:

                        "Silence!"
                        "Silence!"
                        "Silence!"
                        (etcetera.)

the remark

(The tugboat outside
anchored to fog, captainless
waits.)

The cocktail party snagged between
ceiling and linoleum bubbles of its component
parts: the toothy shout, wave, tight lip laugh, —
asterisked to another hour and planet —
eye-closed bongo dancing, the staccato-ed
armpit, when, whoa, the basilisk remark
at the crystal to lip, gashed a laugh
felled a shout to earth, closed a bewildered
eye and stamped all, all and final
to a mottled and fuming bas-relief.

(The captainless tugboat
anchored to fog
waits and, true to promise to Those Who Escape
wheezes its beckoning once. Twice. And final.)

formula for tragedy

Mouse meets cat.
Mouse eats cat.

Washington Square: August Afternoon

to J.M.B.

Crouched over and across from the waiting girl, (dabbing nail polish where nylon hell broke loose, and realizing fully for the first time there is no way to really repay the rich, unless it's a kind thought now and then) her impatience crackles the sound of orange-colored cellophane.

crouched over and across from the door TO LET where glass "I" slipped,
the visage of the little boy, deceived, misinformed at the bend in the path. He found his bush. Spectral-peeing-(suddenly grown, and WOW!-snarled in a Gidean discourse-whizzing, the fly zips, the visage vanishes.) Tomorrow's fertilizer, the good and bad of all;

crouched over and across from the newspaper sniffers,

the poet who gave up the middle class, upper and lower, as hopeless (sprawled on the fertilized French poodle grass scorched brown; he, not the class, for security insults, melody embarrasses.) Too early risen, weighed down by The Rosey Eclipse, he hears the sound within his head of The Nail hammered into hardwood and knows, allez oop, the day beckons. He throws back his head, the head of a stunted rooster (no, not at all like an alley cat) he trumpets and challenges the day with a deliberate cough, ppplllttt! and "Hopeless! Hopeless!" He's found his song; he saunters off to someone's sparrow roost called home, so small it holds nothing but pocket editions.

Crouched over and across from the thread winders,

the "Here comes the sightseeing bus! Stick out your tongue, do things," the scent and music of anemone on the breeze up from Wall Street, sashaying, (tempting one to say he wears ribbed velvet and not corduroy), the Porcelain Boy upholds the emblazoned reputation the rouged tourist clipped with the Greyhound visa. Categorized and catharized, the spot is X'd on the margin.

Crouched over and across is N.Y.U.

from Harlem: Sidewalk Icons

Man, in some lan
I hear tell, tears wep
in orange balloons will
bus wide open with
laughter.
        Aw, cry them blues Man!

The Infant

The quagmire of an overstuffed sofa---
　　　　the shin is for kicking the cat is for
　　　　skinning the stick is for sticking
this is just the beginning: the snowsuit inferno.
　　　　Earth and stairs they leap ice bites hot
　　　　water bites wind bites the bite of the
　　　　white she-wolf is broken glass. Red means
　　　　HURT. The sun is a splinter for the eye
　　　　lollipop is . . .
horehound suspiciousness.
　　　　Cheeks mean love but duty is a pee pot.
No outlines of day are left uncrayoned in dreams.
They mean MORE:
　　　　I want. Shin for kicking cat for skinning
　　　　stick for sticking
this is just the beginning
　　　　I want.

Tango

Broom, broom, man of a broom; Valentino-slick lurking overly-casual cornerly in the realm of the potted palm. He awaits his opportunity with the oblique awareness that launched the Vikings, that killed the cat.

"Vo do do dee-oh do?"

There is gigolo black beneath the guise, you don't fool easily.

Floor, floor, coquette of a floor, Cupid-bowed and boyish bobbed, wrestling with a nervous desire, crosses the planks of her legs, a craven recrossing, and smacks away on her Sen-Sen to beat the holy banjo.

"Oh, DO! sweet pappa."

"Dee-oh do do?"

"Oh, tweets!"

"Dee-oh do do do?"

That's all. The tango is on!

"Oh, suggums! what you're doing to my seams and crannies!"

A curtain of tweet-tweet, tweet-tweet, tweet-tweet.

The floor rolls over in place, spliced and sufficed, sweating her little puffs of dust; indeed, in a different state. The tango is ended, the cat is killed, tableau vivant.

But where is broom? (He was asked to leave Shanghai, North Africa, and Outer Mongolia, but now rumor has it he's living happily ever after in Staten Island.)

Nothing is ever where we left it!

The Iconoclast's Closet

Holding the last of his old-found toys, he subjects himself to grim inventory which he makes whenever a son is born. The close quarters of the closet of his mind, to alien nostrils has the smell of fever and the sound of gurgling in sewers.

First, the reactionary is gouache. There! There he sits, his graystone face chiseled with Brahmin hands, behind a long black desk, on a swivel chair that never swivels. His dictionary has one word: NO buttered out generously to everybody everything everyday. His mind is a curved line starting at void ending at vacuum tripping over raspy negatives all the way. Gray hair and little cabbages are growing from his ears. One day, in a whistle voice, he said: MAYBE. Clarions blew in large rooms! Shimmying eucalyptus, shattering the tombs! A stallion ran wild into the horizon and the sun rose high on a new gray day. And from The Sitters favorite kidney a mite-y sprout grew;

second, the prayer houses. Above the chants, organ and sputterings of the blindly devout in the service

Service, the most impressive elements are the silences.
These he has preserved in a glass ball;

third, aris-tuckus-y;

fourth, marriage. Marriage, the shopgirl's technicolor dream, the dream of the heir to the nuts-and-screws millions married to the heiress of the dynamo zillions; marriage, the dream of the poorgirl already two months gone, and the nightmare of the woman valiantly scarred;

fifth, bits of paper; credos, documents, agreements, treaties, all labeled

scratched out, rescribbled, tucked away in a vest pocket.

(He knew none of these things when.)

On closer observation we notice the closet isn't a closet at all. His house had been bombed like all the rest. Ideals are taught early in life; thereafter, right on through to the deathbed, experience nullifies one ideal after another; so many bombed statues to the left and right of the paths. With his chain of keys is a bottle opener; this is the key to his kingdom. So we see, the closet is really an outhouse.

In a moment's pause, he turns to face his day.
Not below, not above, but directly ahead. I suspect there are few among us who can exchange, transmigrate, and see his day as he . . .
Interrupted, he interrupts: "I see the day before myself, and I am true to it. Fill in your days; go racing across your worlds on squeaky crutches." The cry of a new born son heralds the day; the iconoclast returns to his inventory.

Silence; it exalts us with its rareness.

TOM POSTELL

Gertrude Stein Rides the Town Down El

to New York City

Then colors rose through the leaves in light
        surprise.
The last peacock poised and sighed on the leaves
        and rose.
Wonderful day careens while blighted riff-raff
        children skate and
Laughingly dig the hole for the mid-western
        bonfire.
Wrap honey in velvet air and hide it in October's
        searching breath.
The bonfire dwindles as the circus leaves and
        the animals roar.
It's only in the sun that madness splatters into
        joy . . .
Cover down the moon for the night before you
        lift the skirts of a cloud.
Love knocks on the inside of my skull and kicks
        in my stomach.
A doe licks the gum from a tree and runs into
        the woods.
She lets me govern her gaze when the parade
        blares its colors.
Gertrude Stein is long dead but under cover rides
        the torn down El.

I Want a Solid Piece of Sunlight and a Yardstick to Measure it With

Seventh Avenue fills at noon with a gray tide of
        suits come out for air.
Noon catching fire peeks over the high rooftops
        and spits into the saloons.
The brown buildings drip with wilting plaster and
        the mighty pigeon's dung.
Sylphindine Fifth Avenue trips on red and green
        lights and slides quietly by Central Park.
Honeysuckle leaps over the hedges as the people
        leave Staten Island for work.
Long Island slides in its channel groaning under
        the new load of grinding storms.
I see the Brooklyn Dodgers on Times Square with
        their bats and balls practicing.
Let us enter the redundant oasis which rips of
        jungle beats on glasses of gin.
We never get on the train that stops to let the
        morning messenger in.
And with rats digging in the cellar the basement
        cement crumbles as we rise.
Lakes of icy whispering trees float crunchingly on
        under the glory of wide blue sky:
O give me a solid piece of sunlight and a yardstick
        of my own and the right to holler.
I don't need to ask for the moon cause I love some-
        thing that melts in your breath.

harmony

We who stung stone know how our toil bathed us in ash, while the lilies of the land covered their heads and shuddered. We had grass blades for legs and tree limbs for arms and our mouths were big black clouds, which at times would burst warnings to civilizations.

We remember the times we were nearly human, and almost understood the caresses of fried fish laced around our groins by ambassador girl diplomats from the sorry state of God.

You and I were the wine glass tasting the wine but swallowing none. Sitting in the forgotten table of love. We looked in our own eyes and blinked stars the moons were jealous of.

I loved you under the crushing sledge of wrath, of morning's pressure on the heat of evening. Moons and secrets.

NORMAN H. PRITCHARD

Magma

hollow or filamentary or silled
in which of these can hold a grasses rock
stock and fallow stretching broad
the chord stung she could run
scotch hipped to her never left alone
wants herselves for the ever was come
to these sprawling among the dialed
pent up upon where no one
will have ever noticed
these daisys pending the sun for it's fall

Asalteris

change
as
circumstance
may   be
of   curious
courses
as
though
as   if
were
in
dubitably un
certain ones
are
n't

From Where the Blues?

Stacks of paperbacks
against whiteless walls
foliate the landscape
of the incubal inclosure.
Above, at the perimeter
of my left eye, curtains
hand siennaed by the neglect
of other importances.

A rueful "Pierrot"
looks downward from his
clipboard perch as if easled
too long in this pagan pasture
where Bacchus boards and Coleridge
no doubt would have lengthened Kubla Khan.

"The Lady" utters a cantata in "praise"
of morning heartaches . . . one more chance
to realize that it's   the unsung
that makes the song. From where the blues?
Strange, this combat that selects its soldiers.
From where the blues? The feeling knows
my ways and stalk them, like the black cat
there, with the yellowed eyes.
I too know the wishing for forgetfulness.

Metagnomy

A mid   the non com mit t e d
com pound s of t he   m in d
an i   m   age less gleam   in g
we at   hers   h aunts as yet   un k no w n
& t   a   u   n   t   s
thru a   c he   mist r y of   ought
t   h at c   hang e   s
c   ours e   s
s   ee   m in g l y
as   if a bird in f light
a   w   or   d
f   or   got ten
in   t   he w   in d '   s w on t

W   h at aim co un s e l s   such   a   gain
un to t he   sylvan d own   of   w   om b s
w   h at   n   ever ever   s   t and
c   a   uses such man   if   est s   t a   s is
to   r   ide   on ly up   on   t h   at move   men
t   he   ear t h   pro   vide s

Of ten the set t in   g m . in d
like d   us k a j   our n   s
as thou g h   the k   now in g
as thou g h   the g   low in g

To s ee k
to   f in d
a l   a   n c e
to   pier c e the   p o s s i b l e

Oft e n a w is h   de   fin e d
like l us t re   turn s
as tho up on an alt   e   r

b l oo d is b   o   k   e   n
as   m eat
is   rite
& a   cc   u   ring   p   aga   n
c   r   u   c   i   fix   ion

E   n   chant   m   e   n   t   s
abo   und   ab   out
the   abysses of   a   m   in   d
oft e   n   b l   in   d   e   d
by   the cat   a   r   acts   of   curt   concern
w   h   i   l   e
aim   s   it   s   daunt   less l   y
on   a   p   e   d   e   s   t   a   l
be   in   g   peck   e   d   up   on
be   t   he   w   in   d   '   S   w   on   t

Gyre's Galax

Sound variegated through beneath lit
Sound variegated through beneath lit
through sound beneath variegated lit
sound variegated through beneath lit

Variegated sound through beneath lit dark
Variegated sound through beneath lit dark
sound variegated through beneath lit
variegated sound through beneath lit dark

Through variegated beneath sound lit
Through variegated beneath sound lit
through variegated beneath sound lit
through variegated beneath sound lit
Through variegated beneath sound lit
Through variegated beneath sound lit
through beneath lit
through beneath lit
through beneath lit
Thru beneath
Thru beneath
Thru beneath
through beneath lit
Thru beneath
through beneath lit
Thru beneath
through beneath lit
Thru beneath
Thru beneath
through beneath lit
Thru beneath
Thru beneath
Thru beneath
Thru beneath

Thru beneath
Thru beneath
Thru beneath
Through beneath lit

Twainly ample of amongst
twainly ample of amongst
Twainly ample of amongst
twainly ample of amongst
Twainly ample of amongst
twainly ample of amongst
In lit black viewly
        viewly
    in viewly
        viewly
        viewly
    in viewly
        viewly
    in viewly
        viewly
    in viewly
        viewly
        viewly
        viewy
    in viewly
        viewly
In lit black viewly
    in dark to stark
In dark to stark
In dark to stark
    in dark to stark
In dark to stark
    in dark to stark
In dark to stark
In above beneath
In above beneath
In above beneath
    above beneath lit
    above beneath
    above beneath

above beneath
above beneath lit
above beneath
above beneath lit
above beneath
above beneath lit
above beneath
above beneath
above beneath
above beneath
above beneath lit
above beneath
above beneath
above beneath lit
above beneath
above beneath
above beneath
above beneath
above beneath
above beneath
above beneath
above beneath
above beneath lit

,

```
"    "    "    "    "
"    "    "    red   "
"    "    "    "    "    "    red   "    "
"    "    "    "    red   "    "    "    red
red  red  "    "    "    red   "    "    "
"    "    red   "    "    red   "    red   "
red  "    "    "    "    red   "    "    "
"    red   "    "    "    "    "    "    "
"    "    "    red   "    "    "    "    "
"    "    "    "    "    "    red   "    "
red  "    "    "    "    "    "    "    "
red  "    "    "    "    red   "    "    "
red  "    "    red   "    "    "    "    "
"    "    "    red   "    "    "    red   "
"    red   "    "    "    "    "    red   "
"    "    "    "    "    "
red  "    "    "    "    "
"    "    "    "    "    "
"    "    "    "    "    "
```

junt

mool   oio   clish   brodge

cence   anis   oio

mek   mek   isto   plawe

WE NEED ---- please read this and see if you
qualify, if you do not care to take advantage of this
please pass it on to a friend.

grown on instead opens the door
a blind went away pulling
large numbers covered with rows
decidedly

toward them some its own
dressed away with the rain
flying in borrowed kind
things in the basket

beside twisted ruddy before
without those mostly or an under
plundered nearly though feasted
delighted so as to be carried

HELEN QUIGLESS

Concert

This garden too pleasant
the moon too near pools
of water avoid

    Reflecting smooth sketches
    of "Spain" in man's desires.

How now brown drummer?
as you hold him in your
spell
    that man of sax
    That princely black
    dreams aloud the
    agony of his race

    and his lips grip
    the telescopic view
    which curves abruptly
    and stares upon their face.

Sailing through the air,
a taloned-shriek
draws blood from the ears.

And long the cry rings

    against stone museum walls
    against city sounds
    against the dying sun's light
    against spiral statues oblivious of rain
    against lily pads and fish of gold
    against minds that concentrate

against love that tolerates
against the multitude
   pale
       so
          that
             smiles

fade
from triumphant sounds of music.

Rings cry the long until
it shudders and dies,

and sweetness comes to him.

ISHMAEL REED

Paul Laurence Dunbar in the Tenderloin

Even at 26, the hush when
you unexpectedly walked
into a theater. One year
after *The History of Cakewalk.*

Desiring not to cause
a fuss, you sit alone
in the rear, watching a re
hearsal.
The actors are impressed. Wel
don Johnson, so super at des
cription, jots it all down.

I don't blame you for
disliking Whitman, Paul.
He lacked your style, like
your highcollared mandalaed
portrait in Hayden's
Kaleidoscope; unobserved,
Death, the uncouth critic
does a first draft on your
    breath.

Dualism
in ralph ellison's invisible man

i am outside of
history. i wish
i had some peanuts, it
looks hungry there in
its cage

i am inside of
history. its
hungrier than i
thot

Badman of the guest professor

for joe overstreet, david henderson, albert ayler
& d mysterious "H" who cut up d Rembrandts

i

u worry me whoever u are
i know u didnt want me to
come here but here i am just
d same; hi-jacking yr stagecoach,
hauling in yr pocket watches & mak
ing u hoof it all d way to
town. black bard, a robber w/ an
art: i left some curses in d cash
box so ull know its me

listen man, i cant help it if
yr thing is over, kaput,
        finis
no matter how u slice it dick
u are done. a dead duck all out
of quacks. d nagging hiccup dat
goes on & on w/out a simple glass
        of water for relief

ii

uve been teaching shakespeare for
20 years only to find d joke
        on u
d eavesdropping rascal who got it
in d shins because he didnt know
enough to keep his feet behind d cur
tains: a sad-sacked head served on a
platter in titus andronicus or falstaff

too fat to make a go of it
anymore

iii

its not my fault dat yr tradition
was knocked off wop style & left in
d alley w/ pricks in its mouth. i
read abt it in d papers but it was no
        skin off my nose
wasnt me who opened d gates & allowed
d rustlers to slip thru unnoticed. u
ought to do something abt yr security or
        mend yr fences partner
don't look at me if all dese niggers
are ripping it up like deadwood dick;
doing art d way its never been done. mak
ing wurlitzer sorry he made d piano dat
will drive mozart to d tennis
        courts
making smith-corona feel like d red
faced university dat has just delivered china
        some 50 e-leben h bombs experts

i didnt deliver d blow dat drove d
abstract expressionists to my ladies
linoleum where dey sleep beneath tons of
wax & dogshit & d muddy feet of children or
because some badassed blackpainter done sent
french impressionism to d walls of highrise
        lobbies where dey belong is not my fault
martha graham will never do d jerk
shes a sweet ol soul but her hips
cant roll; as stiff as d greek
statues she loves so much

iv

dese are d reasons u did me nasty
j alfred prufrock, d trick u pull

d in d bookstore today; stand in d
corner no peaches for a week, u lemon

u must blame me because yr wife is
ugly. 86-d by a thousand discriminating
saunas. dats why u did dat sneaky thing
i wont tell d townsfolk because u hv
to live here and im just passing thru

v

u got one thing right tho. i did say
dat everytime i read william faulkner i
go to sleep.

Fitzgerald wdnt hv known a gangster if one
had snatched zelda & made her a moll tho
        she wd hv been grateful i bet

bonnie of clyde wrote d saga of suicide
sal just as d feds were closing in. it is
worth more than d collected works of ts
eliot a trembling anglican whose address
is now d hell dat thrilld him so
last word from down there he was open
ing a publishing co dat will bore d
devil back to paradise

vi

& by d way did u hear abt grammar?
cut to ribbons in a photo finish by
stevie wonder, a blindboy who dances
on a heel. he just came out of d slang
& broke it down before millions.
        it was bloody murder

vii

to make a long poem shorter—3 things
        moleheaded lame w/4 or 5 eyes

1) yr world is riding off into d sunset
2) d chips are down & nobody will chance yr i.o.u.s
3) d last wish was a fluke so now u hv to re
turn to being a fish
p.s. d enchantment has worn off

dats why u didnt like my reading list-right?
it didnt include anyone on it dat u cd in
vite to a cocktail party & shoot a lot of
        bull—right?
well i got news for u professor nothing—i
am my own brand while u must be d fantasy of
        a japanese cartoonist

a strangekind of dinosaurmouse
i can see it all now. d leaves
are running low. it's d eve of
extinction & dere are no holes to
accept yr behind. u wander abt yr
long neck probing a tree. u think
it's a tree but its really a trap. a
cry of victory goes up in d kitchen of
d world. a pest is dead. a prehis
toric pest at dat. a really funnytime
prehistoric pest whom we will lug into
a museum to show everyone how really funny
u are
        yr fate wd make a good
scenario but d plot is between u &
charles darwin. u know, whitefolkese
        business

as i said, im passing thru, just sing
ing my song. get along little doggie &
jazz like dat. word has it dat a big gold
shipment is coming to californy. i hv to
ride all night if im to meet my pardners
dey want me to help score d ambush

Poetry Makes Rhythm in Philosphy

Maybe it was the Bichot
Beaujolais, 1970
But in an a.m. upstairs on
Crescent Ave. I had a conversation
with K.C. Bird

    We were discussing
rhythm and I said
"Rhythm makes everything move
the seasons swing
it backs up the elements
Like walking Paul-Chamber's fingers"

    "My worthy constituent"
Bird said, "The universe is a
spiralling Big Band in a polka-dotted speakeasy,
effusively generating new light
every one-night stand"

We agree that nature can't
do without rhythm but rhythm can
get along without nature

This rhythm, a stylized Spring
conducted by a blue-collared man
in Keds and denims
(His Williamsville swimming pool
shaped like a bass clef)
in Baird Hall
on Sunday afternoons
Admission free!
All harrumphs! Must be
checked in at
the door

I wanted to spin
Bennie Moten's
"It's Hard to Laugh or Smile"
but the reject wouldn't automate
and the changer refused to drop
"Progress," you know

Just as well
because Bird vanished

A steel band had
entered the room

ED ROBERSON

news continued   release

rescue workers fought today
and yesterday another day today
in efforts to avert the same
tomorrow. one eye witness on the scene
reported and the wide effects
opened a decade in the wrecks
of sequences supposed under control.
official estimates of toll
have been suppressed for purposes of piece
by piece attention to belief.
authorization to the area
is given as is birth to myriads.

poll

skin that is closed   curtain.
it is impossible to know.   how
the light is cast.

a mark that is kept   the elect-
ion determining the race
before the candidate   runs.

darkie is the night is
an old image given color.
the skin is history.the dark horse

Four Lines of a Black Love Letter between Teachers

bored. confused actually. have started several letters.
usually about   4 in the morning whch is to say something
about my tenantcy in the house of sleep/black.
evicted. universal, wch is to say "There is a certain
                        amount of traveling
                        in a dream deferred."
i taught Langston Hughes today. Same In Blues.
and my soul/*stoppt before the mirror at my body sleeping in the white-*
ness of the moon . . .

brought it back.saved   newspaper then lost it
waking up.about the confrontation hate
the loss of meaning in that word) between the black
students and the president   of the campus the folks made him
look like a fool. he is   retreating into his power bag
more jab about in loco parentis do you dig it tsk tsk

there is something about music in this letter. mmm how you do me
this heh way. but the lecture was music   you know
i got so many bags i can only read they faces
from inside.run out   of labels even fore
i run me out of words   wch is to say
/descriptions   there's that refrain again
wch of the wch ways to gone   *and say . . . */black

a classical problem lawd
i/s here by myself
got no company.what i got
/i
already got.what i know
i know
why i bother with puttin it down.nuthin

nobody else know   wch is to say.
all you all/you people why you want it down   this way
i was about to attend a sinkin.when yall showed up with the hole . . .
mmmiss you baby

you ask was it all right. i said yes wch is to say.
i didn't say (to you no.no is not
a pill.quinine nor envoid.yes is.for me.
tastes weird as anything else
about us. put a hair
on my hope chest. but thas oright.
been loving other men's sons lately
buying toys for students' sons on my way to dinner
don't take much to get an A from me.
hey hey you there baby at the end of this line
let me be yo sidetrack till yo mainline come
i can do more switchin than yo mainline
done now   students about presumption."A certain
                              amount of nothing
                              in a dream deferred."

1 Ibid.,
2 vid., next refrain
3 ad int./cf., today is a ♀ . sine loco (:op.cit.,
4 i.e.,i am   watering an irish rose.   ooop pop a dop bop

I've lost the letter of this act.
with a pun as multiple as that.
"theys liable to be confusion."
to write   a love letter for someone else
to you the one i love
is a love   in a where someworld sometime else
done now
so signed if this is the night, who else but but
is it   black
but look/here look here one more
thing.every new love adds   to the meaning of love any lingering old
    [love
has to catch up even to linger. so you're going to have
his black baby

On the Calligraphy of Black Chant

i paid my becoming   well   not to   become
i paid
i paid my becoming
     my becoming
             well
     my becoming well
i paid my becoming well not to
i paid my becoming well not to become
and now gain even to gain my life
and now
and now gain
       gain even to gain
           even to gain my life
and now gain
's a hole
  a hole in the hungry pocket
       the hungry
             gain
's a hole in the hungry pocket of my skin

and all points between those two are points
and all points
and all points between those two
and all points between those two are points
points opened
opened in that skin
opened in that skin and closed there
opened in that skin and closed there
                       one way!
opened in that skin and closed there one way.
the opposite of bleeding   one way:
and any shot   either life or last of thieves
's the opposite of bleeding

is the opposite of bleeding and not healed
                              and not healed
and not you
              i am the sieve
and not you
              i am the sieve
                              and not healed
and not you i am the sieve
                              and not your friend
              i am the sieve
                              and not your healed
and not you i am the sieve and not your friend.
              i am the sieve and not your friend
              i am the sieve
              i am the sieve

it must be that in the midst
of any tonal language there is a constant huddle
of all substance's matters

where any accident of sound
could speak and
the sound of people's walk
talk   chicken with your head pecked

is their baldhead heels
in the midst of a song another
song   and any doing sing its work
song

if i must think i must think
i must think well

this is to demonstrate
i must think
my meanings are tonal

the bell ringing
from the well

in the long line i must think
it is tonal
i must think well

it is tonal   too/much
as this is rhythm

        walk talk chicken wid yo head pecked
        you can crow w'en youse been dead

      walk talk chicken wid yo head pecked
      you can hol' high yo bloody head

like
we haven't lost much
language   but not music as speaking/the drummer walking on his
hands

any moment   (12/4/69   4:30 A.M.
chicago

the open door and oh no
and the wish it wasn't
murdered in its sleep
its wife and soon baby
thrown by the police
into your turn
to see the maybe
home open the door oh no

american culture   is the pot
calling the skillet black. american
even as a mulattoed
culture is very deeply colored. folks

white america is an unconscious black
brother culturally to black americans
as though still in a blanched coma
from the burn

that

chuck berry's
elvis presley charlie mc carthy
was actually a dummy.
it said what he said
and made you move your head
yes

that
nigger is the man.

even black people had to
read it in translation to be sure
it was that hot a star they saw
the wise men coming
toward
themselves. had to read its
hips
because in europe they don't talk that.
not 'till turkey
at least.

A. B. SPELLMAN

the beautiful day, V

he went
to the window.
it folded & shrank.

quietly, & without warning
them, night leaked into the
room, into the "idea" of the group.

how easy it is to lie
to you. what a soft
lie your silence is.

she moved closer
to the window, night
shifted & sank.

john coltrane
an impartial review.

may he have new life like the fall
fallen tree, wet moist rotten enough
to see shoots stalks branches & green
leaves (& may the roots) grow into his side.

around the back of the mind, in its closet
is a string, i think, a coil around things.
listen to <u>summertime,</u> think of spring, negroes
cats in the closet, anything that makes a rock

of your eye.   imagine you steal.   you are frightened
you want help.   you are sorry you are born with ears.

the twist

a dancer's world
is walls, movement
confined: music:

god's last breath.
rhythm: the last beating
of his heart.   a dancer

follows that sound, blind
to its source, toward walls, with
others, she cannot dance alone.

she thinks of thought as
windows, as ice around the dance.
can you break it?   move.

Blues: My Baby's Gone

my baby's gone
& incredible distances close before me
my face pressed up—side the wall
which doesn't open a window
into a room of dead flowers
dead tokens of the hours
i spent with my baby

my baby's gone is not like a song
like a rope i could swing on
wind on my shades blurring faces
in the park to streaks of color
in the dark while the singing
rests my chest from the hurt
that fills the hole in me
my baby left.
it's more a cry like an answer
a twist in the turning
a sobering of skids and
a panic of drugs

my tongue dries up & manhattan collapses.

Did John's Music Kill Him?

in the morning part
of evening he would stand
before his crowd. the voice
would call his name &
redlight fell around him.
jimmy'd bow a quarter hour
till Mccoy fed block chords
to his stroke. elvin's thunder
roll & eric's scream. then john.

then john. *Little old lady*
had a nasty mouth. *summertime*
when the war is. *africa* ululating
a line bunched up like itself
into knots paints beauty black.

trane's horn had words in it
I know when I sleep sober & dream
of sun & shadow, yet even in the day john
& a little grass put them on me clear
as tomorrow in a glass enclosure.

kill me john my life eats
life. the thing that beats out of
me happens in a vat enclosed
& fermenting & wanting it to explode
like your song.

                    so beat john's death words down
                    on me in the darker part
                    of evening. the black light issued
                    from him in the pit he made
                    around us. worms came clear

to me where I thought I had been
brilliant. o john death will
not contain you death
will not contain you

The Truth You Carry Is Very Dark

it is not spoken to him
who has bled salt
but to him who lives within
the Penumbra of the Silent Mind
upon this shadow
cast the shadow of the wind
thicken the Penumbra with the vision
that God is what we know
that what we do not know is the same
that truth is what we touch
if it is there
if it is not there

PRIMUS ST. JOHN

All the Way Home

The lamps hung like a lynching
In my town.
It was a dark town.
In a dark town,
Light is a ragged scar.
Fright begs that ragged scar.
It begs doorways.

I love that town.
From its lean men
I learned
Emotion;
And how to hold that fine edge,
That makes us
       people . . .

Mrs. Blackwell's
Sold her house.
Since her husband revolved his head,
She wears bright hats
That speak to people.

B.J.'s doing time.
His children betray that time,
By the breathing it takes
To dream through windows.
Mary Lee dreams him letters;
She dreams by heart . . .

Now I feel a new scar.
I've left home
And leaned so far,

I'm almost zero.
And though it's lonely
Whatever knowing is;
It strings a long fine wire.
At night I lie awake
And listen to that wire—

All the way home.

Benign Neglect / West Point, Mississippi, 1970

Suppose you were dreaming about your family,
And when you woke up
You found a man named Sonny Stanley
Had just shot you (5 times),
Or justice
Looked just like the color your blood was running—
Running wild in the world—
But the world wouldn't see.
Then
You read, somewhere
(I think it's the papers)
If it's a problem, Boy,
We don't have one here
We don't ask a man to die
Like groceries babbling froth to flies.
But bleeding,
You watch your neighbors
Write away to their windows to
Hide! Hide!
    "He's not there. He's not there."
The last sentence?
The last sentence is your *Father*—
One of the windows . . .
    "He's not there. He's not there."

Goodbye, Johnny.

The Violence of Pronoun

1

Loving came her way,
        vicious.
It rose up,
From the earth,
And made her father's hand,
Around her throat,
A bird of prey,
And carried her away—
        In mind,
Like a limp patient.
He was not drunk.
It is worse.
In this world,
We cannot feel . . .

2

In my sociology class—
        For understanding
Black folks—
They tried to understand
Our homes—
        Like buckshot.
What we have done,
        To love
Is unforgivable.
They took out rakes,
And treated us like dirt.
It was so perfect
They asked for grades.

3

Leaving people out of this—
I can forgive.
I married her, anyway
And in the church,
When I unfolded her hand,
                    I saw

In her palm
The way she would die . . .
Leaping out of democracy
Through some weird window
                    white
With the wilderness of God—
            1965 Memorial Day.
And I went on, crazy
            at first,
And crazy even now
For being so unmilitant . . .

4

What I told that class,
(You know) they said it hurt.
"It is our innocence
That makes us vicious."

Studying

American Lit. is beside you—
Keep up—
By a small cup
And smaller words . . .
It is night—
By tin cans of light
About the river
You are faithful . . .
But where does it go,
Which soul,
Slanted roof,
Bolted door . . .
There is absolutely nothing here,
But the very late birds,
And what you are.

GLENN STOKES

Blue Texarkana

the whaling backdoor of Texarkana
    back there in the old
cottonfields back home
    back in the garden
of the gruesome descent
  to the hay shed and potato
peels the invisible highway
         And fall
    of the high gods
                  from Jackson to Selma
to wine bottles on a back
    wooden porch and moonshine
crystallizing on dust on mantel
pictures of old dad and poor mama

who flipped out popping
questions into my discriminating head
    because the clay was too Red
    in Columbus that spring so
Injuns rose from the gullies
and slipped knives between my
    aching shoulder blades
    making love mercy black-eyed pudding
steeple-chased milk and contraceptives
to curve overproductive minds
    and turn black molasses to weak wine
    potato wine on my uncle's back porch
his flesh bubbling at the mouth
in their pond which reflects everything
    hidden and usually obscured
    never seeing dusty Texarkana and
    fudge-faced pie with death

on their hands
it was Texarkana hell
and southern belles ringing in my
    ear drums I hated
    could not stand found my love
    thrusted down
    down down
my gasping throat

to think to know to guess
that home they died a
thousand whaling times on trees
    tombstones broken chimneys of grass
    brick and dust porch tracts
    mosquito heaps their carcasses
laughing not being "human"
they died we forgot but
cannot filter from our bloods
    the trueness the arrowness
    lying in this closet-shaped town
    we cannot remove the stink

CECIL TAYLOR

Scroll No. 1

Whistle into night
Recognize exorcism
    blue's history.
Whittled whispers while
city technique wrung
    awakened needs.
Spring cotton answer
    Recognition
    Carver's oil estranged
    outer earth's garments
    Scorched exclusivity
    Shining Bandanah
Thru ground mounds and
    honeysucklevine scraped
    dust rises. Noon dimples
    sweat titty.
Bugle brow browned
Indignation laments
Yellow childrens
    scampering ass'n
    pigtails stompin'
    rag-a-mom
            White crucifix
            White flame
            White God
            White hood
            White white
            White which
            Pains shame
            Call your'n
            Happiness born
            comin' onto

Whiteness
Greased bolts
Mud fields
Hot stream
Stung stank
Stitch sanguine
Satiety sought
Surreptitious
Seraph
Sin sinning
Singing song
Set 4 centuries long
Mirror born color squared
difference excuse
mountain organ hill hill
tongue tastes
Tar flesh trampled seeds.

Scroll No. 2

Nation's lost diplomacy
lost notions duplicity
Demagogic democracy
Damned dutiful
Darned cloth
blue serge   white white
one someone   shirt floptic
tank bat and "yeah bo"
I'ma Senatah!
You just sing dance unseen
    crophandler
    food maker
    lost nobles
    chewed spit'n
    grits shit and
    molasses hot smellin'
    teeth toothless
    hyeena smile
'Ah is so happy
Youse mah master
    ooh ooh ooh
Kick me again   gin
    Prick Duster sperm
Ground life out
Chambers red
Redolent
Lao Vaudois
    leaves bow
Swollen gulls mate
exigent whimpers
swimmers duck
rockfall legion's
            asleep

where bonnets
bent whore's lost
puerility romps
unchided over
back roads black
in night cesspools
to constellations
        stranger
Justice invisibility
impenetrable
lighted masks
calcimined mimes
ejaculate polyglot
systoles
Dry cell of money
has locked the minds
and cauterized hearts

Da
Phallic mystère
never speaking
stems grasp's lightning
  air thru whole
     socket
mayhem
      turn
    lighten'd
    soft
        To You
       then
        in
       some
     sounding parafin
   arms are raised rose seed
        in sun
        burnin—
Dark night vacant shadows peep the
borrowed friend arms extend
       upward
        elbows angled
       somethin' dime Tin'e
      an ear lak, those
      ever readied, roost
             slick'n.
Hewé-zo
   vertabraes seam'd atolling
   meteor pa-zzanin a hissing
   asson adorn bells past
   a 2nd month lain 7 side.
            churn/

Da
oldest ancestor/ fertilized seed
    / making LegBa
    / phallic mystere/
         by the
         center post
         of Peristyle

Choir

1.

of time as horizontal paths
fed sea agglutinizes
field (phasoun) verticles plowed
discover inner vision
soil and river sound
weight'd margins invisibly
functioning anchors in flight
agglutinized space thus absorb'd
        scatter'd deposits
thoughts: so many drops of rain
        transposed heritage
mirrors at will turn backward
        differentials in organization.

1a.

Agglutinized space cursed bough
supporting sky
        Bess between Nut beneficent
protective function of
twins magically born inn eigh Astral
        scent paths read 7 colors round
nape o'time
layers lit retain moist syllable befo'
cyclical imprint
        ly dampen'd tongue né breath beat
a full
space agglutinized self differential in
organic
        cross fertilization of registers
        oral & visual reconstruction

feeding bark, feeding sea
        twins
     Face of kings.

                                    2.

of node tightly bound in cave
juice from reed metamorphosed
transferr'd root differentials
in time lay flatten'd palm
across upturned heel
compendium loosens wig
press back the grain being thaw'd
I'se field, I'se rock, I'se time
holdin back rain agin' mountain
hidden in concrete entombed
square joints of rusted steel
hold the saffron ray nebah less
than arrange gold float an eye
face morning stretch'd & held

                                    3.

            between animal glut
            transferr'd tusk
            these be minimal gesture
            ambivalent transparencies
            cloud'd cloths distemper'd
               to obfuscate.

                                    3a.

        elusive street carry indomitable
        shadow spit consequence risen
        fluted was but trunk transposed
purpose gleams undaunted
perpendicular
blood altar'd wood spray wind'd vowel
cometh

bud blown circular to the blessed skin
analogous
ear from continuum light draw matter to
bone
become dress'd skin talk'in syllabic
monotone hidden from passage walk
ovah
delta thru crystal charged atmospheric
ray illumined by irridescent 3 points
root necessarily a continuing echo
weighted margins invisibly beating

4.

face worn reflect upon inner vision
time of rivers continued intelligence
the fall rises lac stalk unknown point
of departure of rain of perimeter
focus accumulated thrusts receiving
"mind" get bounce, scent lifts echo
—Painting horizon bees street walker
cross fertilizing moving registers
scattered deposits being sons of light
Preparation reverb anacrusis
ritualized triangle essential
spirit waters waded hidden cycle alone.

4a.

of space particular node
betwix layers announce
savor'd victuals in rapped
basin resonate climbin' growth
salvage time establish'd
area agglutinized abyss
being Astral & all registers
between.

LORENZO THOMAS

Inauguration

The land was there before us
Was the land. Then things
Began happening fast. Because
The bombs us have always work
Sometimes it makes me think
God must be one of us. Because
Us has saved the world. Us gave it
A particular set of regulations
Based on 1) undisputable acumen
2) carnivorous fortunes, delicately
Referred to here as "bull market"
And (of course) other irrational factors
Deadly smoke thick over the icecaps,
Our man in Saigon   Lima   Tokyo   etc   etc

Embarkation for Cythera

And out of the solitude
Voice and soul with selves unite

                                        C. Okigbo

This color, its pure absence
in other words a space
            some African mothers, children
cupped in their slim arms
They are bending into the sand
and it is their lesson written there.
            A new motif of
                        destruction—
The idea of a written language
                        When before,
the words in our
            mouths were enough.
      Not that it takes anything away
from the people we are,
                  "Education"
You don't write "corn" if you
            mean okra.
Along Merrick Blvd, standing in front
the dance hall
                  it's the same thing, the
      cop in a luminous blue
His badge spreads all over his face,
threatening me. There should be
                  Someway to get in without paying.
                  Rain that falls into the dusty
                  Life of the people on
the street, it turns into a new language
All the fine mommas walking inside,

getting out of Grand Prixs
          Can hardly read
this paper without stumbling over "embarkation"
What someone has done to us, that
                    my words become unintelligible.
It says, do not despise your own
                    I wonder if they see that,
All those foxes.   All of a sudden
I'm so glad I have on my wide
pants, my 10 dollar banlon shirt
                    The girls wish I was
inside, too. At least, I think so
                    This much is understood
I go down to Benson's Burgers
                    and sit in the parking lot.
Food smell, but I don't have any money
          All I have is the blues
and a ticket for someplace called Cythera
a bus outing on Sunday.
          Got this magazine telling about the great
                    new thing going on in Nigeria
                    and I have my beautiful high
a green alcove of the evening
                    called "music"
My voice when it is understood,
          Piped into dancehalls and restaurants by
this very intricate and lovely machine.

Song

You asked me to sing
Then you seemed not
To hear; to have gone out
From the edge of my voice

And I was singing
There I was singing
In a heathen voice
You could not hear
Though you requested

The song—it was for them.
Although they refuse you
And the song I made for you
Tangled in their tongue

They wd mire themselves in the spring
Rains, as I sit here folding and
Unfolding my nose in your gardens

I wouldn't mind it so bad

Each word is cheapened
In the air, sounding like
Language that riots and
Screams in the dark city

Thoughts they requested
Concepts that rule them

Since I can't have you
I will steal what you have

Twelve Gates

Face it. The stars have their own lives and care
They are forced into it by your other eye and
Opposite side of your thoughts. Who takes sides
The world quite as fashionable as liars imagined

The picture of one fragile girl in an avalanche
Of the kimono required for their soft trade.
Who is so daring at first to draw lines in the sky
Dingy with this neglected daylight. Opened fan.
Life itself is such a simple thing and we need it

Then here comes the music again. And we need that too
People asking each other. The invention of reason.
And those who own nothing what of those walking around
Without land, without cash value, properties. Without

Nothing in their name. Whose destinies
Are not marked or marked down. What of
The ones who are meant to rise in the world
By their names. Whose names are not known.

These worlds are lost in a minute only a gem
Of substance remaining. The necessity to change the form.
These streets clothed in an atmosphere of ash and care-
Less emotion. Who are these persons roll their shoulders

Outside the window in starlight and streetlight
each young man there reminds the girl of someone
These are the last words I send you for awhile.
Written across her fan. Her open eye all flame and
You can feel it take shape in your eye. The lines.

Sufficient confusion calls for a song and
The figure with how many sides. Holler.

Once to the ocean. Sing it for the woman
Whose hands open and deliver the dream

Arousing itself from the day's laborer walking
These streets back from the edge of the river
Deep into town. Traffic. Your voice plays across
The street on the curb right into my open hand

The Bathers

We turned to fire when the water hit
Us. Something
Berserk regained
An outmoded regard for sanity
While in the fire station
No one thought of flame
Fame or fortune did them

We did them a fortune. We did
Them a favor just being
Ourselves inside of them

Holy day children

In the nation coming your children will learn all about that

But the water creep about us
Water hit us with force.
We saw a boy transformed into a lion
His tail is vau the syllable of love
A master before fellow craft
The summit of the Royal Arch

Lotus. Mover on the face of the waters . . .

Sleepless Horus, watch me as I lie
Curtained with stars when ye arise
And part the skies. And mount the Royal
Bark

They said the ancient words in shameful English
Their hearts rose up like feathers
In the hidden place

And Horus step into the flood of noon
Shedding his light upon the worlds

It was in Birmingham. It happened.

Week after week in the papers
The proof appeared in their faces

Week after week seeing the same moment grow clearer
Raising the water,

Filling the vessel. Raising the water.
Filling the vessel

O electromagnetic Light shadûf!

Ancient hands bearing water
Ha

        The star broke
      Over the tub

       All righteousness

Not deceived by sunshine nor the light
From a man's desire

Deceived by desire
So that in the moment
The people cast light from their bodies
"Light" being the white premeditation

The simplest fashion
What they want is light

Another source to equip
Their dry want

Want fire light. Space light
Discretions of neon

At least.   So to appear natural
          Where the sun is

360° of light

Consumed in the labors of comfort
That cries for the balm

        Of all that is natural
   Desire.

Bathing in the dark
The water glowing
In the plastic curtain
Suddenly heated

As another expels past satisfactions.
cold as she washes gas tears
From her man's eyes. We hate you.

Hot on her soft thighs
Like the dog's breath at noon by the Courthouse

We hate you for that

   But ancient hands raised
This water
As the street's preachers
Have a good understanding hear them

      O israel this O israel that

Down here in this place
Crying for common privilege
In a comfortable land

Their anger is drawing the water
Their daughters is drawing the water.

Their kindness is laving and
Oiling its patients.

     That day
       The figures on the trucks inspired no one

Some threw the water
On their heads.
They was Baptists

And that day Horus bathed him in the water
Again

And orisha walked amid the waters with hatchets
Where Allah's useful white men
Came there bearing the water
And made our street Jordan
And we stepped into our new land

Praise God. As it been since the first time

Through the tear of a mother

Another Poem in English

John Donne would think of an island
After all this noon is written
All afternoon I think of several
Words

        change   ribbet   foment   format

Plan   plane   solder   alchemy   Army

    leads   you're kidding   gaoled

  Corsica   desire   solidarity

insular front   font   Louisiana   Rumania

The execution of light

Known also as peace about being
A serpent twines itself around space
Wanting to call this that. Really

I'm doing that anyway!
Anyway, I'm doing that

And this this

Dark Laughter

Veldt Village,
O
globe of thatch palms and idols of the tribe,
how many times,
how many tales,
alive with the lore and ethos of
lionhearts and hyenaloins,
foxlivers and eaglebeaks—
now nest, like tropic birds, among
thy straws and leaves,
thy rushes and reeds,
without a trope,
without a logos,
to disturb
anonymous dust?

In
Veldt Village,
dark laughter
sparkles, in spangles
of light and noise and smoke,
at the idée fixe of
a dark Don Quixote or a dusky Tartuffe.
Dark Laughter
flashes Rabelaisian humor
in gross caricature and visceral naturalism
of the élan vital.
The Good Gray Chief had given
the ear of wisdom to the Elders
as proverb and fable and parable
ascended the ladder of
commedia de figurón,
comédie larmoyante,

which foot-loose travelers find
from palm to pine.
"Elders," he said, "if I could be born again,
I'd ask the gods to make me a bard.
Tonight we have with us two bards, one black, one white,
whose feet have left their spoors on distant shores;
from them, therefore, I want to know
<u>what</u> land the Great God has blessed
with the strongest wine!"

The Zulu bard,
born on the veldt but
bred on a hill above the Seine,
straddled the question with
<u>ethnic two-ness</u>:
"Like Tennyson's Wanderer,
much have I seen and known—
in Montmartre cáfes, swilled
the liquors of many lands:
rye, bourbon, rum, gin, vodka,
brandy, arrack, and a score of native wines,
from Dakar to Cape Town;
yet, O Mighty Chief, I cannot swear
what land has the strongest wine."
The applause <u>de rigueur</u> of the Elders arrested
like the inner digit of a dog's hind foot,
the Good Gray Chief
lanced the black bard's ego
with a glance and a sneer:
"The loins of a straddler cry for a kola nut!"

The graybeards
bellylaughed and clapped
their thighs
and then turned on their alien guest
a Leyden-jar battery
of quizzing eyes.

The vagabond poet
from Greenwich Village,
via the Latin Quarter,

winked at the Zulu bard,
his boon companion of auld lang syne.

For the first time in years,
A Long Way from Home,
sung by the ancient cook in the family kitchen,
stirred the dregs of nostalgia.
"O Mighty Chief,"
the expatriate said,
"I was born and bred a Kentucky mountaineer—
and my grandpa had a still in a canyon hideaway."

. . . A memory image hied its way . . .
in a speech not for Buncombe,
his old buddy from Asheville had said
in Greenwich Village,
"Look homeward, Angel"—but
"You can't go home again."

The poet said:
"My grandpa bootlegged liquor in
the County Courthouse
when the Law tried to make the USA
a Sahara."
The Elders finessed patterns in their beards,
as the stranger's candor snailed across their minds.
The poet
thought:
Who doesn't like the juicy roast
of a story snatched from
the spit of life?
The graybeards chewed it,
speculatively.
(After all, didn't a white man cook it?)
They smacked their lips.
"My grandpa used to put
rattlesnake heads in his kegs.
Only God Almighty knew how much power
my grandpa's white lightning had.
Old timers said his liquor burned
a blood-red path

from the tip of the guzzler's tongue to his lowest gut!"
The graybeards,
their eyes a white anabasis,
palmed their paunches and groaned.
"Elders," said the poet,
"one day my grandpa gave a rabbit
a swig of white lightning
and turned him loose.
What do you think the rabbit did, Elders?
Well, he turned a somersault seven times,
like a Big Top acrobat,
and then staggered right up
to grandpa's prize hound dog,
spat in the old champion's eye,
and said:
'Mr. Hound Dog,
please, oh, please, don't try to block my way.
When I lose my temper,
hell itself belches forth fire and brimstone!'"

Dark laughter
exploded
like
a Molotov cocktail
against
a caterpillar tank.

Good humor notwithstanding,
a people must keep its weather eye open:
the God of the Whites has a hand that breeds
seventy-seven sleights.
The Elders upheaved their beards
to the hubris-symbol of the tribe:
The Good Gray Chief bowed to his guest,
his crotchet up his sleeve.

"In truth, you are a bard,"
he chuckled.
"Your fable is a tribute to your land.
Now, since other peoples
tonight

have neither bard nor chief to speak for them,
it remains for me to take up the fallen spear.
The issue narrows:
<u>*it is*</u>
Africa versus America
to see
which has the stronger drink—
the stronger men.
Remember, O bard,
your rabbit, after all, challenged only a dog
to test his heart, to test his guts!"
Suddenly his eyes became
as soft as a shedding crab.
"O Bard, the pity of it, Bard!"

In the tropic night,
the Elders stirred
hand and foot,
leaned forward,
taut as tom-tom skins.
The Good Gray Chief continued:
"As the eldest of the Elders,
my memory now conjures a tale,
shuttling between what <u>is</u> and what <u>was</u>.
One day my grandpa gave his favorite monkey
a swig of his most powerful palm wine.
The beast danced a jig,
pounded his breast,
shrilled his defiance at Elders and gods;
then,
like an eagle's flight of wit,
fled into a jungle
which concealed a man-eating lion
that had defied the tricks
of the bravest warriors.

"The monkey staggered
hither and thither,
hit and miss,
beating
shrubs and bushes and underbrush,

terrifying
beast and bird—
shouting
at the top of his lungs:
'Mr. Lion,
O
MR. Lion,
don't try to hide from me.
I'm going to bring you in,
dead or alive!' "

Dark laughter
was the roar of a sirocco
churned out of the Libyan deserts,
bound for Malta.

After the chuckles had died
in the last ditch,
the American poet horselaughed and said:
"Elders, your chief got
that dead-or-alive stuff
from a USA movie in a ghost town of the Old West!"

The Zulu bard protested with a grin,
"Are you accusing the Good Gray Chief of theft?"

"Poets know all men are thieves,"
the Westerner said,
as his hands swept right and left toward the horizon.
"After all, it's One World—isn't it?"

In
Veldt Village
dark laughter
beguiles the tribal censor,
cheats the governess, reason,
with Falstaffian relief from stock responses to
paramount chief and witchdoctor,

[unfinished]

The Chitterling King

I

<u>With Whom the Die Is Cast</u>

Professor Alpha Umphers
D. Sc.,
an ebonite Basilius
on his Siaitic see
as president
of the Afro-American Academy,
although his lectern is awry in the dissent
of masks, bestirs a hair
neither in the dawn of his porcupine goatee
nor in the dusk of his leonine pompadour,
for the cataract in his inner eye shuts out the debris
of ologies and isms Teneriffe
shovels into apple-of-Sodom December;
<u>that</u>
that snaps open his synapses
is the ill-omened spots on the dice he remembers:
the die of Caesar
at the Rubicon,
before the Ides of March stained Pompey's statue;
the Emperor Jones,
ague-
ridden by Little Formless Fears of Acheron,
as Jeff, the Banquo porter, on his haunches rolls the bones
of Armageddon
in the Great Forest's shadow;
and the craps of Catfish Row
vermeil-veiled like the glow
of scarlet-ariled logs
on firedogs.
Though sense peeped from the metaphor

— a fat crab scringing from a shell —
like gill-net fish, they felt
the unknowable bore away the bell.

His mind a shuttlecock for days
between its yes and no,
Dusty Busby at last
let his ballad go
upwind to Windus.

The Chitterling King's
Egeria,
Miss Lou McGee,
gasped
at "Chittlings" in
the ballad's title, turned
as yellowish-green as she-
ironbark, and clasped
a pouting-pigeon breast,
and rasped:
"Illiteracy!"

As Mr. Windus snailed through his mail,
he gave his tie a ritualistic pat,
flicked the ash from his coat-of-arms cigar,
bull's-eyed his mirror wastebasket, spat
into the crumpled-horn MS.
from the ex-star
of the Chocolate Bar.

In a marijuana dream, on Mt. Usura
an ebony swellfish-bellied boss,
to the rhythms of The Chittling Blues,
nailed Dusty Busby to a cross!
When Banker Nicodemus Cahn's
gold spinner was cast from Sugar Hill,
Ezekiel, reimagining a hornet's nest
of slights
grew hotter than a kiln;
but Mrs. Ursula Cahn's

Picadilly-Creole smile,
contrived like a Macy model's,
was the silken guile
of a geometric spider; so
(opposite Ezekiel, on this occasion)
she played again
the prima buffa in
Of Flies and Men.

A too-big mattress, his buttocks
overslopped the Chippendale;
unmindful that he cracked Priscian's head,
he was himself the cicerone: FOR SALE
upstarted from his one-
acred personality
like Oceola's plume of glory
at a scalp dance:
the root of evil has no self-irony.

As aborigine's shadow a swagman's trail,
reporters from the ANP,
the Harlem Black Dispatch, and Ebony
gathered to angle the sesame of success;
but with a Bismarkian grimace
as a diamond tooth headlighted his face,
the Chitterling King,
pillowed on his swivel apogee,
recalled an idol and said: "Gentlemen,
it's an enigma wrapped up in a mystery."

II

By Whom the Die Is Cast

As Ezekiel Windus performed the chitterling rites
in Major Patmore's Stonewall Jackson House,
a Caedmonian vision vibrated across his mind
like the silhouette of a flittermouse;
he siphoned the image off his chef's routine,
and then among the pots and pans he heard

a voice that isolates curd
from whey pipe, pipe, "Ezekiel!"

Ezekiel saw de wheel
'way up in de middle of de sky,
Ezekiel saw de wheel
'way up in de middle of de sky;
little wheel turn by faith,
big wheel turn by de grace of God,
'way in de middle of de sky!

His eyeballs blurred, as if from rheum, then cleared
miraculously; but rigor mortis froze
the anatomy of his unborn word.
Unmistered, he shook the dust
of blind-gut Horeb, Georgia, from
the hog-trough of his number thirteen shoe:
a Percivalean bum
unmewed by beggars of life,
he wolfed his mulligan stew,
as if bulimic,
among outcasts of Poker Flat
in Hoovervilles heroicomic
but this
is the higher all' ottava of that:
Like crabs scrawl to gulfweed
in the Sargasso Sea,
the footloose ragtag sought,
beyond the tide crack of reality,
the roc's egg
in Guy Tabu's Casino & Barbershop;
here, no man had to make a leg,
and none became emeritus;
from Tchaikovsky to Bebop,
from Marx to Jesus,
ists and isms ran the gantlet of pros and cons:
this was the Walk, the low-brow's academe;
no censor threw a rabbit punch,
and every disputant was on the beam.

Yesterday, in <u>that</u> place,
the <u>Nous</u> was Plato; today, in <u>this</u> — Guy
. . . but he was more . . .
he was the Cassius
who answered the wild prayer, the wild cry
of Ezekiel when, his arms anchor-lead-heavy, he sank
— not in the Harlem but the Tiber —
like a weary brogan in a snow-dust bank.

One black-frost dawn,
Guy leaned against the double-bolted door,
a solitary potter wasp, and eyed
Ezekiel, who, as if a sammier wried
sweat from his skin, hunched on the floor
cleaning brass spittoons, humiliation
boring into his core
like a sewing awl. Guy read
the Georgian's mask, then scraped
his shining spot-ball head.
Rusty Busby snored the boozer's snores
into the billiard-green. Ezekiel's broom
push-pushed across
the ultima Thule of the gambling room
as Guy Tabu, ex-actor of the Harlem Opera House,
pooh-poohed his vamped-up vanity:
"O Son of Ham, how can you make your mark
in the little old Sodom of New York
without the address of Sir Success
or a black-leg's city map?
Alas, O Capon Sap,
who d'you wanta be —
The Great I Am,
Kneepad Amen,
or Flip-Flop Sam?"

Guy snatched the broom and huckled his hip
and mopped the sweat that didn't drip
. . . push-pushing . . .
until he reached the cliosphinx of the wall;
then, then, his feigned

bull-donkey labor drained
his all in all.

"Push Alley is a dead
hind-gut," he said;
"to thine own self be true,
and it must follow . . . thou canst not then
find the address
— Lord, black man, Lord! —
of Sir Success
on Pull Avenue
and Bull Boulevard!"
Negro weeklies in ads
from coast to coast
keystoned the ebony Quesnay's boast:

WINDUS CHITTERLINGS WEAR THE CROWN
of Free Enterprise
and Business Renown!
EZEKIEL WINDUS
Has Now No Peer!
Salute
NEGRO BUSSINESS' MAN OF THE YEAR!

A neon trademark
skyscraping on Seventh Avenue
forefingered and screamed:

IF YOU ARE BLUE
WINDUS VITAMINS
WILL JACK UP YOU!

The Windus curia regis
baited caste and class and race,
as the wings of an Aberdeen gold spinner fly
cheat the rainbow trout or the calico bass;
bourgeois palaces
and proletarian shacks
refracted dissonances of kind:
the scene might alter . . . but behind

it Windus remained the Thrax
readied for the arena's sands;
while, with red-inked stacks
of ledgers, dark Insuls performed
clog dances on Sisyphean skids,
Ezekiel Windus piled up dollars with the gusto
of a Ptolemy erecting pyramids.
Sloe Gin Hornsby, like a midwife,
watched Rusty Busby revamp the news
in a ballyhooing ballad epitheted
<u>The Chittling Blues</u>:
<u>If the little wifie says you ain't</u>
<u>the man you used to be,</u>
<u>let Windus chittlings pep up</u>
<u>your sub-vitality</u>
<u>with vitamins A & Z</u>!

No laughs in the Casino:
a begging friar from Ireland,
he waited, his fabling hand
hoboing along the strings; and then
his gaze bent up to eyes awonder
with awe that filmed the maiden Zeppelin.

Guffaws cataracted:
Rusty Busby,
in crescendo
without
diminuendo,
volleyed the strings and minstreled:

<u>Listen, black, and listen, tan,</u>
<u>listen to this guitar-man,</u>
<u>Windus chittlings, boiled or fried,</u>
<u>are 100% A-mer-i-can.</u>

Sloe Gin Hornsby, a honky-tonk
pianist fumbling for a flat
to posit after a clef, finally sharped,
"Betcha Windus would give a grand for that!"

Applause
quick like a knee jerk — but
Sloe Gin
spooned out the "Blues"
and "ain't"
as maggots in a work
of Art. A hydra of views!
Sloe Gin
beheaded the monster
with the Excalibur
A Psalm of Life!

The Casino rife
with antimasks, Dusty Busby sought an od
to vigil the Note and Word,
An Aaron's rod
with almonds. Sometimes
a twit-twat bard below the peak,
by lucke or wisedome,
riseth with the eagle Greeke.

"Sloe Gin," Dusty Busby dealt his blow,
"a note-maker ought to know
an Art idea
with the gonorrhea!
An artist is a bird, a very strange bird,
that puts a nest together
in tune with the time, the place,
the weather;
at its worst or best
every nest
is different
by the way a feather
is tucked or a straw is bent!"

III

For Whom the Die is Cast

As the scholars of the Afro-American Academy
crosshackle Dr. Woolf,

the rack and pinion of Professor Umphers' memory
send back and forth,
back and forth,
swivel shuttles
that weave spot figures
with nuances of irony
in the fabric silk
of <u>finesse</u> and <u>geometrie.</u>

A <u>dance macabre</u> along
a broken Everglades' levee swirls into his mind:
a mock moon with a mockbird's song
above the black debris and yellow carcasses
puked from geyerine morasses;
He tries to blind
himself with liquor, but a moccasin,
whose coil-spring lightning
barely fangs past his shin,
sobers him, makes him aware of rats, opossums, dogs,
cattle, wildcats, horses, coons, chickens, hogs,
refugees, black and white — tragedies
without a M. Champollion, agonies
in an untranslatable tongue:
a dark man with his skull
pulped by a pistol butt
and arms outflung
like Him,
dying;
a pale, pale woman in travail,
crying
a cry
interpreted by
young Umphers
as <u>Why</u>
<u>hast thou forsaken me</u>?
. . . this, <u>this</u> . . .
as alligators, bull and cow,
instinct with the necessity
of Now,
couple in lacerating ecstasy.

Bristle-faced like a dealer
forced to ante
for the next jack pot,
the etcher shei
watches egg-mite hours pass
toward dark of dawn
and designs, on the glass
of young Umphers' greenery,
a Rodinesque patriarch
(blacker than cypress lawn)
tearing
apart the ifs and buts,
baring
the raca's scars beneath the inner shirt,
staring
at the tiger's raccroc stitches
that unite the net-ground pieces
of the Why that bitches
philosopher and fool,
beyond the yellow sapphire
clusters of the faggot fire.
When the Chitterling King glided by
in his aeried limousine —
the Deuteronomic Law
of cars — every oyster eye
on Seventh Avenue upcocked in awe:
the jim-crow law inverted, the chauffeur loomed
blonder than
the blondest Aryan
the D. A. R. ever saw —
blonder than the dehaired maw
of an opossum
to be
braised golden brown,
to a T,
by black mammy,
for the F. F. V.

The nordic's livery
vied with the court regalia

of a Hapsburg duke; and when
the anthracite Vanity-fairian
of Harlem's Belgravia
put foot on ghetto dust, pedestrian
homebodies forgot
the Very Lights,
while the O-mouths
of gadabout skites
edging round
froze like the open doors
that neither shape a shadow
nor a sound.

Neither vicars of God nor the Chitterling King's,
and unaware of glazas and sugar cane,
the gazers achieved an echoic zing
by linking <u>I's</u> in an ethnic chain.
Before he whiffed marijuanas
in a coral-red ribaldry,
before he saw his I-ness fold
like a jack crosstree,
Rusty Busby
spotlighted
with his guitar,
voodooed skulls of the black and tan
in the Chocolate Bar,
as a scop at wassail
in Heorot with Hrothgar
witched the brains
of jarlmen and thanes.

<u>I play any game
that you can name,
for any amount
that you can count.</u>

<u>If my luck is up,
if my luck is down,
I'm the Mr. Barnum
of this Black Man's town</u>!

The ghosts of van and taxi vanished in the ear,
like falling diphthongs. Ezekiel's push-pushing
a school boy's bushing
the asses' bridge,
Rusty Busby
grew darker than a ridge
oak, inside and out,
for fame had vapored like St. Bruno's lily;
so out of a mood in tune with rhythms of the broom
a ballad flowed like water willynilly:
God's golden slippers
give the angels the blues —
I ain't got no corns,
'cause I ain't got no shoes!

I was once a gentleman —
had a two-timing gal.
I was once a square-shooter —
had a Judas for a pal.

I gave once the public
a brand-new deal;
but I got in the rear
of an ass's heel!

Gonna load them bones,
gonna stack them cards;
so come up to see me
in the House of Lords!

Ezekiel used the unholy three
— push, pull, and bull —
to make his chain splice of reality
. . . below — fangs that never say adieu . . .
. . . above — beaks that never say good-by . . .
the frog (Rusty Busby) in a bog
(Even as you and I)!

The big wheel moved by Faith,
the little wheel by the Grace of God:

<u>a wheel in a wheel</u>
<u>'way in the middle o' the air!</u>
Ezekiel felt Tabu's Casino cant
probe his flesh and drain
the arrogance of his arm,
like a severed basilic vein;
yet he had plasma to cere his yesterday
and light a candle to spirit scruples away.

Booker T.'s
"Let down your bucket where you are"
and the Fisk Jubilee Singers'
"Who Will Be a Witness for My Lord?"
became bubbles breaking
in a buckaroo's discarded gourd,
or phantom swishes
of Shakespeare's untraceable sword.

The decade had its ups and downs,
like the heads and rumps of giraffes
in a single file; and the polysyllables
of Harlem bellylaughs
acidified the pottage on the shelf;
but Ezekiel's laugh had the golden oxytone
of Success itself.

The Hand of the Chitterling Empire,
with the riddle of a recipe,
held dominion from palm to pine;
the filmed farms of the Windus Company
(as well as sources hid in redtapery)
shipped delicacies of swine.

In spite of ambush bugs
whose bile
cartooned a Jew in the $-pile,
"What we say and what we do,
at this time and in this place,
will digit the high- or low-
watermark of the Race."

The belly of his memory gripes:
"I'm lynched in effigy
by the Harlem Black Dispatch,
and the blackamoor Reds nickname me
Uncle Tom Gobineau
in the <u>Daily Worker</u>; but
I know and know I know
Nurture is only a C-3 nurse whose pillows prop
up Nature's invalid — Old Man Flop!"

Dark laughter crackles like the rinds of roasted pork
in the unction of the pothunter's spiel;
but Professor Umphers has the one's-own look
of a ginner when the teeth of the wheel
draw the fiber through the grid:
the pier of vanity
has no ice apron; but he
filters off as fiddle faddle
the notion that a prefiguring ice-blink
haunts the bridgemasters who think
the genes of a monastery pea
load the dice of destiny.

To him, the darkness, fore and aft, outside
a man's parentheses,
is but a keg's unminded lees:
he puzzles out the filets d'Arachné,
the X's no magic circle has denied,
and the Bredoyean dice cast with naiveté.
unaware,
he held as fetish the Balzacian <u>de</u>;
hobodom's democracy
was an incubus blurb
blaring a blue
false indigo cacophony;
so he withdrew
beyond the Paul Pry eyes of the bums
as the male orang-utang of Borneo
retires to the upper fork of a tree
when the female and the kids disturb
His Magnifico.

Venetian oars create
a cadenza of love;
but the Dixieland wheels of a gondola,
an antiphon of hate:
a black Ulysses of the underworld rods,
he tailored for himself the schedules of
earthquaking
Atlantic Seabord decopods
coupled to dinosaurian cars
— bellying freight —
engulfed in vaporscape
from steam-hissing thoraxes
escaping;
he watched, stalk-eyed, Waldorf-Astorias
pancaking
to coppiced passengers
and baggage-wagon loads
. . . like dragonfly cruisers . . .
forsaking
Cloud-Cuckoo-Land roads.
In the sea dust of pros and cons,
old Dr. Vachel Woolf upanchors to his feet,
despite fleshpots and honorific years;
his temper puckers red with heat
blooms, and his frown out-Molochs Moloch's
in Pandemonium's council among his Peers;
and as he shakes his ebony Bola boa-headed cane,
the Harlem Opera House is thunder-girt with cheers.

"Nature or Nurture, that is the question,"
he narrow-throats,
as if to watch the vertical strokes above the notes
of a jazzer's staff;
but his sarcasm clicks with the precision
of a facsimile telegraph:
" . . . Well . . .
the genes will tell.
Every Afro-American knows
a Bilbo cannot keep
the black <u>Invictus</u> in Yazoo bilboes."

He pegs Professor Umphers with a glance
as nib-edged as a fishing lance
from a bully tree;
and then he ravels out the skein
of Mendel's ism and Galton's ology.

The hearers sit like prick-eared priests before
bronze caldrons, at Dodona's terminus,
echoing winds heigh-hoing
up Mount Tomarus,
while Dr. Woolf
presents his hatti-sherif in a voice as ominous
as low barometric pressure:

[unfinished]

GLORIA TROPP

Poem for Ernie Henry

paint my crib a
                     land of grass. . . . scarabs & mariposas
holy hour
               in the city . . . in the aisles of oil & perfumes
my lids part the people dressed in strings
                           wearing tensions
                           making dances come through
                                longing
GOD'S SELF of straw of straw burning on both
                              ends
                          WHAT! WHAT! WHAT!
and WHAT foot glides through days that are ONE SCREAM
                      LOUDER THAN THE NEXT
Body light making blues offering
                     under a low range of sky
and other blues
               in a coat. . . . that dims blues ears
and WHAT WHAT for my blues. . . . .
                      all the world that's
                                    a
                                 tree

engraved on the cheek of facing
                 this hard stone

TOM WEATHERLY

first monday scottsboro alabama

they don't hold grudges
bridges that don't know cars
are in this century.
they don't know better to
ride over wooden bridges
wagons from shotgun ridges
bridgeport, paint rock, sand mountain
they ride to county courthouse
square to honest trades of
samplers, plowshares, shotguns
bloodhounds, homebrew & gossip.
they come to buy back issues of time
from north alabama ridges
over bridges sherman didnt burn.

Canto 7
first thesis

for m.l.k., jr.

aim   get your sights & its sound
in abstract or journal movements
to a peace settlement

old western fancy

dude shot my man

dead,
     precious lord blow off
theres no willy in th blues theres no you.

vocal texts evoke
abode adobe
edens popes blest
turnt holy trope
local cross aglow

fishes
theirs fit
people fidget
taught theirs fulfil
wishes lies & fitful dreams.   070599.
                                    (For Jane Zvi Kimmelman)

"gandhabba" #5

thomas mouths
smooth mythos.
medusa
seemed amused.

"croatan"

entelechy
and bicycle
too bucolic

we cultivate
in colony
the accolade.

Canto 10
wooten

th black hat stingy brim
on th street you live
one more day wearing it angel
enuf so you live. Enuf.
Devil lights up th day knowing
which hat to wear in his
green avenue stompers above franklin
going downtown, th robins
by stuyvesant, nostrum, utica avenue.
our wireless "robins nest" slim harpos
blue thang. do your thang blue sea
cop the reefer   ride away
th highs translate literally
railway carmens soft white underbelly.

p.w.t.

for miss kitting

linda June put your white dress on
when black dark falls full moon rising
shadow of moonseed owl, fog
slow catfish swim low tide rising

san francisco mean fog rising.

Contributors

Lloyd Addison published and edited the small press journal *Beau Cocoa* and was a member of the Umbra group of poets. Born in 1931, he was the author of *The Aura and the Umbra*.

William Anderson first contributed "There's Not a Friend Like the Lowly Jesus" to the anthology of African American poetry *Dices or Black Bones*, edited by Adam David Miller, where the poet advised readers that "the only relevant biographical information about himself is that he is a poet, journalist and novelist."

Russell Atkins, born in 1926, was a mainstay of the *Free Lance* magazine and workshop located in Cleveland, where he still lives. His collections include *Here In The*, *Heretofore*, *Phenomena*, and *Objects*. Paul Breman, whose Heritage Series of black poets published Atkins, recently published 7 @ 70, a pamphlet by Atkins celebrating his seventieth birthday.

Amiri Baraka's (LeRoi Jones) many books include *Preface to a Twenty Volume Suicide Note*, *The Dead Lecturer*, *Blues People*, *Black Magic*, *Reggae or Not*, *Transbluesency*, *Funk Lore*, and *Somebody Blew Up America*. He was born in 1934 and has served as the New Jersey Poet Laureate and has been honored as the Newark Public Schools Poet Laureate. He has released numerous recordings of his work, including *New Music / New Poetry*, *It's Nation Time*, and *The Shani Project*.

Jodi Braxton was born in 1950. She has edited the poems of Paul Laurence Dunbar and is the author of *Black Women Writing Autobiography* and *Sometimes I Think of Maryland*. Early in her career she performed her poetry in concert with saxophonist and composer Marion Brown.

Harold Carrington maintained a widespread correspondence with poets through the duration of his jail sentence in New Jersey, which led to his publication in a number of significant magazines and anthologies. None of his work had been published in book form at the time of his tragic death in 1964 shortly after his release from jail. He was only twenty-six years old.

Stephen Chambers's "Her" first appeared in *The Journal of Black Poetry* in 1969.

Jayne Cortez is the author of *Scarifications*, *Mouth on Paper*, *Coagulations*, *Somewhere in Advance of Nowhere*, and *A Jazz Fan Looks Back*. She has produced a number of landmark poetry and jazz recordings, the most recent of which is *Borders of Disorderly Time*. She was born in 1936 and spent much of her early life in the Southwest before relocating to New York, which has been her home since.

Lawrence S. Cumberbatch contributed the poems collected here to Orde Coombs's 1970 anthology *We Speak as Liberators*.

Rudy Bee Graham published poetry in *Negro Digest*, *Black Dialogue*, and *Black Fire*. Two of his plays were presented at the New Lafayette Theater. He was among the contributors to the landmark Black Arts anthology *Black Fire*, which was edited by Amiri Baraka and Larry Neal.

William J. Harris's books of poems are *Hey Fella, Would You Mind Holding This Piano a Moment*, and *In My Own Dark Way*. He is the author of *The Poetry and Poetics of Amiri Baraka: The Jazz Aesthetic* and the editor of *The LeRoi Jones / Amiri Baraka Reader.* He was born in 1942 in Yellow Springs, Ohio, and currently teaches at the University of Kansas.

De Leon Harrison has been a writer, film-maker and a painter. A long-time resident of the San Francisco Bay area, he co-founded Cinema Blackscope. He was born in Arkansas in 1941 and taught at San Jose State University.

David Henderson is perhaps best known as the author of a very successful biography of Jimi Hendrix. One of the central figures in the Umbra group of poets, his collections include *Felix of the Silent Forest, De Mayor of Harlem,* and *The Low East.* After many years in California he returned to New York, the place of his birth in 1942.

Calvin Hernton, also of the Umbra group, was the author of *Sex and Racism in America, The Sexual Mountain and Black Women Writers,* and the collection of poetry *Medicine Man.* He was born in 1932 in Chattanooga, Tennessee, and died in 2001. He was writer in residence, and later a professor, at Oberlin College, from which he retired in 1999.

Joseph Jarman has recently rejoined the Art Ensemble of Chicago, a world-renowned group of musicians with whom he has worked for more than three decades. His poems and recitations can be found on several of the group's recordings (including *Fanfare for the Warriors* and *A Jackson in Your House*) as well as on his own productions. He is the author of *Black Case* volumes 1 and 2.

Ted Joans is the author of *Teducation, Afrodisia,* and *Black Pow Wow.* Born in 1928, he was also noted for his painting and his collage works. He was perhaps most infamous for his "Rent a Beatnik" ad in the *Village Voice.* Ted Joans died in 2003.

Percy Johnston was born in 1930 and was a founding member of the *Dasein* group of poets and a central figure of the Howard University Poets. He was the author of *Sean Pendragon Requiem* and *Six Cylinder Olympus.* His life-long interest in philosophy is evident in his *Phenomenology of Space and Time: An Examination of Eugene Clay Holmes's Studies in the Philosophy of Time and Space.* Percy Johnston died in 1993.

Stephen Jonas wrote *Exercises for Ear* and *Transmutations.* His *Selected Poems* were published posthumously. He was a frequent contributor to *Yugen, The Floating Bear, Measure,* and other journals of innovative poetry. At least three different years of birth have appeared in print. There is little doubt that Stephen Jonas died in 1970.

June Jordan's books include *Things that I Do in the Dark, New Day, Passion,* and *Naming Our Destiny.* Her prose works include *Civil Wars* and *Soldier.* A Harlem native, born in 1936, Jordan was raised in Brooklyn. She died in 2002, still working as a popular professor at Berkeley, where she organized a number of important public poetry projects.

Bob Kaufman founded the notorious *Beatitudes* along with Allen Ginsberg and others. His books of poetry include *Solitudes Crowded with Loneliness, Golden Sardine,* and *The Ancient Rain.* While much of Kaufman's life is shrouded in mystery and rumor, often self-perpetrated, there is some certainty that he was born in 1925. He died in his beloved San Francisco in 1986, upon which occasion then-Mayor Diane Feinstein declared Bob Kaufman Day in the city.

Elouise (Hanna) Loftin is the author of *Barefoot Necklace.* Her poetry can also be heard on the recording *Celebration* by Andrew Cyrille. She was born in Brooklyn in 1950.

N. J. Loftis is a poet, novelist, philosopher, and film maker. His books include *Black Anima, Condition Zero,* and *Love Story Black.* He was born on the south side of Chicago in 1943. He completed a Ph.D. at Columbia University and has taught in the city university system of New York.

Clarence Major has long been recognized as a major American poet and novelist, and he is also a painter. Collections of his poetry include *Swallow the Lake, Cotton Club, The Syncopated Cakewalk, Symptoms and Madness,* and *Inside Diameter.* Among his many prose works are *My Amputa-*

tions, No, All-Night Visitors, and *Emergency Exit.* Born in 1936, he lives in California, where he has taught for many years at the University of California at Davis.

Leroy McLucas (Lucas) is a photographer and filmmaker as well as a poet. His photographs of jazz artists and writers appear on album and book sleeves, and he was the photographer for the book *The Shoshoneans,* which he published with Edward Dorn.

Oliver Pitcher published a collection of poetry, *Dust of Silence,* with Troubador Press, who were also the printers for Baraka's journal *Yugen.* He was also a playwright and his work *The One* was included in *Black Drama Anthology.* He was born in 1923.

Tom Postell was a central figure among the community of black artists in Greenwich Village at mid-century and was an early contributor to Amiri Baraka and Hettie Jones's magazine *Yugen.*

Norman H. Pritchard was a member of the Umbra group, and the author of *EECCHHOOEESS* and *The Matrix: Poems, 1969–1970.* He was born in 1939 in New York.

Helen Quigless, a native of Washington, D.C., studied with both Robert Hayden and John Oliver Killens. Born in 1944, she is a graduate of Fisk University. She was a contributor to such important anthologies as *For Malcolm* and *The New Black Poetry.*

Ishmael Reed, a widely-recognized novelist and essayist in addition to his work in poetry, is the author of *Conjure, Chattanooga, Shrovetide in Old New Orleans, Mumbo Jumbo* and *Yellow Back Radio Broke-Down.* Reed was born in Chattanooga, Tennessee, in 1938 and is a long-time resident of California.

Ed Roberson has published *When Thy King Is a Boy, Atmosphere Conditions, Etai-Eken,* and other books of poetry. Born in Pittsburgh in 1939, he now lives in New Jersey.

A. B. Spellman is probably best known today for his book *Four Lives in the Bebop Business*. His collection of poetry *The Beautiful Days* was published by Poets Press in 1965. Spellman was born in 1935, has taught at Morehouse and Emory Universities and has worked as an administrator for the National Endowment for the Arts.

Primus St. John, the author of *Skins on the Earth, Dreamer, Communion*, and *Love Is Not a Consolation: It Is a Light*, teaches at Portland State University. He was born in 1939.

Glenn Stokes first published "Blue Texarkana" in *We Speak as Liberators: Young Black Poets*.

Cecil Taylor is among the key figures of the new directions in jazz beginning in the 1950s. A noted pianist and composer, he often includes his poetry as a part of his jazz performances. Taylor was born in 1929 and began playing piano at the age of six. He studied at both the New York College of Music and the New England Conservatory before beginning his long and prolific recording and performing career.

Lorenzo Thomas, another Umbra alum, has published several books of poetry, including *The Bathers, Chances Are Few*, and *Dancing on Main Street*. He was born in 1944 and was a longtime resident of Houston, Texas, where he taught at the University of Houston—Downtown. Thomas died on July 4, 2005.

Melvin B. Tolson is an important link between the poetry of the first half of the century and the more radical poetics of the second half. His books include *Harlem Gallery, Libretto for the Republic of Liberia*, and *Rendezvous with America*. He was also a noted dramatist, debate coach, and lecturer. The poems included in this collection have never been published before. He was born in 1898 and died in 1966.

Gloria Tropp is described in Amiri Baraka's *Autobiography* as appearing at readings "made up like in Hollywood science fiction movies about what blacks will look like in the future." Her live performances of her poems quickly became legendary, and her future is upon us. Her poem in tribute to musician Ernie Henry first appeared in *Intrepid #4*.

Tom Weatherly is the author of *Maumau American Cantos* and *Thumbprint*. He was born in Scottsboro, Alabama, in 1942 and studied at both Morehouse and Alabama A&M. For many years he taught a writing workshop in New York that attracted some of the most innovative younger poets. He now writes under the name "Weatherly."

Acknowledgments

The editors wish to record a special note of thanks to Jelani Wilson, who undertook the initial efforts of researching permissions for this collection. For additional assistance in securing permissions, we wish to thank Hampton University, Loyola Marymount University, and Pennsylvania State University. A deep debt of gratitude is owed the special collections staffs at U.C.L.A., the State University of New York at Buffalo, and the Moorland-Spingarn Library at Howard University. In particular, the editors thank those extraordinary poets/collectors E. Ethelbert Miller and Michael Basinski.

And if we might make a rare break from our unified editorial voice, Lauri Ramey would like to say that no undertaking is imaginable without the advice and encouragement of her husband, Martin Ramey, nor would it be anywhere near as much fun. To which Aldon Nielsen adds that he would be unimaginable without Anna Everett, who has lived with and contributed to this project before we knew it was a project.

Poems from Lloyd Addison's *The Aura and the Umbra* are reprinted by permission of Paul Breman.

Poems reprinted from the journal *Yugen* appear by permission of Amiri Baraka.

Poems by Jayne Cortez, copyright 2003 by Jayne Cortez.

Poems by Percy Johnston are reprinted by permission of his literary executor, Walter DeLegall.

Poems by June Jordan, copyright 1971 by June Jordan, reprinted with the permission of the author.

Poems by Bob Kaufman are reprinted with the permission of Eileen Kaufman.

All poems by Elouise Loftin are reprinted by permission of the author: copyright 1972, Elouise Loftin, and copyright 2003, E. Hanna Loftin.

Poems that originally appeared in the collection *Dices or Black Bones* are reprinted by permission of Adam David Miller.

"Paragraph from English Speaking World" copyright 1963 by Clarence Major. "News Story" copyright 1965 by Clarence Major. "A Petition for Langston Hughes" copyright 1967 by Clarence Major. "Media on War, or the square root of vietnam" copyright 1970 by Clarence Major. "Edge Guide for Impression" copyright 1965 by Clarence Major. "A Poem Americans Are Going to Have to Memorize Soon" copyright 1970 by Clarence Major. "Not This-This Here" copyright 1970 by Clarence Major. "Mortal Roundness" copyright 1970 by Clarence Major. "Pictures" copyright 1970 by Clarence Major. "Water USA" copyright 1971 by Clarence Major. "Education by Degrees" copyright 1974 by Clarence Major. Poetry by Clarence Major reprinted by permission of the author.

Poems from Oliver Pitcher's *Dust of Silence* reprinted by arrangement with Brayton Harris of Troubador Press.

Permission to reprint poetry from Norman H. Pritchard's *EECCHHOOEESS* granted by New York University Press.

Poetry by Ishmael Reed reprinted by permission of the author.

Permission to print unpublished poems by Melvin Tolson granted by Melvin B. Tolson, Jr.